ICELAND SUMMER

ICELAND SUMMER

Travels along the Ring Road

KURT CASWELL

Illustrations by Julia Oldham

TRINITY UNIVERSITY PRESS
SAN ANTONIO, TEXAS

Trinity University Press
San Antonio, Texas 78212

Copyright © 2023 by Kurt Caswell
Illustrations copyright © 2023 by Julia Oldham

Book design by Anne Richmond Boston
Illustrations by Julia Oldham
Author photo by Rachel Veale

ISBN 978-1-59534-269-0 paper
ISBN 978-1-59534-270-6 ebook

Trinity University Press strives to produce its books using methods and materials in an environmentally sensitive manner. We favor working with manufacturers that practice sustainable management of all natural resources, produce paper using recycled stock, and manage forests with the best possible practices for people, biodiversity, and sustainability. The press is a member of the Green Press Initiative, a nonprofit program dedicated to supporting publishers in their efforts to reduce their impacts on endangered forests, climate change, and forest-dependent communities.

CIP data on file at the Library of Congress
27 26 25 24 23 | 5 4 3 2 1

In memory of Barry Lopez, who urged me to go and see,
and for Taylor, my heart

All journeys have secret destinations of which the traveler is unaware.
— Martin Buber

This is an island and therefore Unreal.
— W. H. Auden, "Journey to Iceland"

Hornstrandir

Ísafjörður

Brjánslækur

Stykkishólmur

Reykholt

Borgarnes

Mosfellsbær
Þingvellir

Gullfoss

Reykjavík

Vik

Iceland

Dettifoss

Akureyri

Egilsstaðir

Vatnajökull

Höfn

Contents

Where the Pillars Washed Ashore   1

Walking to Laxness   14

On Not Looking into Snorri's Pool   23

Eating the Pylsur of Heaven, Part One   31

Eating the Pylsur of Heaven, Part Two   40

Let's Take the Bus, Part One: The Neatnik   48

Into the Hornstrandir, Part One   58

Into the Hornstrandir, Part Two   68

Into the Hornstrandir, Part Three   80

Let's Take the Bus, Part Two: The Sleeping Giant   89

The Dizzying Heights of Dettifoss   98

Waiting for the Monster   109

Let's Take the Bus, Part Three: The Mariner   120

A Visit to the World's Only Penis Museum   128

The Troll Wife's Mountain and Other Stories   136

Behind the Doors of the Árni Magnússon Institute   148

That Day on Viðey   161

Acknowledgments   171

Notes   173

Where the Pillars Washed Ashore

REYKJAVÍK, AND AROUND

If we go somewhere on foot, we know the way perfectly.
— Chögyam Trungpa, *Meditation in Action*

t was raining in Reykjavík. The rain popped and gathered and ran in little lines down my rain shell to drip onto the sidewalks as I made my way through the streets and along the storefronts. The sky came in low overhead like the ceiling in some middle-class American house built just after World War II, and I could see mountains across the bay that rose and vanished into smoky clouds. I had nothing to do that day but wander the streets in the rain, where the cool onshore air from the North Atlantic came in over my face and hands. I felt alert and awake and fairly happy, as you do when you come into a new country, even after a long series of flights with the various mishaps and annoyances of fly-ing—the cramped seats, the disappearing food and beverage service, the high price of checked bags, and the unpleasantness of being locked into the slipstream of a major airline's whims, which (at least to a passen-ger flying with modest funds) seems to be a system set up for the sole purpose of ruining your day. Coming into this bright country—bright because what light there was was scattershot from cloud to sea—I knew that this first impression of the place would persist in my memory for as long as I had one.

Reykjavík felt more like a village to me than a city. Not because of its modest population (120,000 people or so) but because it faces inward on greater Faxaflói, the city's bay, looking onto Mount Esja and that mountain's correspondence with the great white tower of Hallgrímskirkja, the Lutheran church up on the hill. The city's orientation gives it a sheltered, if not homey feel, even as you cast your gaze outward onto the bay, and on a clear day you can see all the way to Snæfellsjökull, snow-fell glacier, on the far end of Snæfellsnes Peninsula. This sense of the near and far, coupled with the clean streets and general tidiness of the buildings with their colorful metal roofs, the freshness of sea air, and the smart-looking easiness of Icelanders walking the streets, their mostly bright and friendly faces, endeared me to the place right away.

The well-known story of the founding of Reykjavík, which warrants mentioning, is that in the latter part of the ninth century, the Norwegian chieftain Ingólfur Arnarson sailed into the vicinity of Faxaflói and tossed his high-seat pillars overboard, proclaiming that wherever the pillars washed ashore, he would build a settlement. High-seat pillars are the ornamented wooden poles once placed on either side of the seat of the head of a Norse household. Of course, nature, not providence, was mostly at work here, as the pillars would be brought ashore by oceanic currents, indicating good moorage for ships. Arnarson set up a temporary camp and sent his men out (probably slaves) in search of the pillars, which they found three years later (that's what you call stick-to-it-iveness). Arnarson named the place Reykjavík, Bay of Smokes, after the steam he saw rising from nearby thermal vents. The most commonly accepted date for this event and so the start of permanent settlement in Iceland is AD 874. Iceland was uninhabited by humans at that time, except for a few Irish monks (encamped and quietly worshiping their god) who, refusing to live among Norse pagans, fled when Arnarson arrived.

For a thousand years since Arnarson's landing, travelers have looked to Iceland as a place of exotic beauty and things wondrous and strange. That list of travelers includes Joseph Banks; Sir Richard Burton; W. G. Collingwood and Jón Stefánsson; Frederick Temple

Hamilton-Temple-Blackwood, First Marquess of Dufferin and Ava (or just Lord Dufferin); William Morris; Mrs. (Ethel) Alec-Tweedie; W. H. Auden and Louis MacNeice; Bill Clinton; Beyoncé and Jay-Z. Lord Dufferin, who traveled here in 1856, published *Letters from High Latitudes* the next year, a collection of the letters he posted home to his mother during the voyage. To Lord Dufferin, Reykjavík appeared to have "been fished up out of the bottom of the sea." And looking outward from the city, he wrote, "the bay of Faxa Fiord is magnificent, with a width of fifty miles from horn to horn, the one running down into a rocky ridge of pumice, the other towering to the height of five thousand feet in a pyramid of eternal snow, while round the intervening semicircle crowd the peaks of a hundred noble mountains." Mrs. Alec-Tweedie, a British writer, artist, and philanthropist, chronicled her 1886 journey in *A Girl's Ride in Iceland* and found Reykjavík "quite imposing" after visiting so many of the hamlets that characterize Iceland. Alec-Tweedie caused quite a stir back home when traveling about the country on horseback, riding astride as Icelandic women did instead of sidesaddle, as was the accepted norm for women in Britain. Collingwood and Stefánsson, in their 1899 book *A Pilgrimage to the Saga-steads of Iceland,* called Reykjavík "a town that strikes one as rather forlorn, and hardly picturesque, though interesting to the new-comer, with a kind of world's end interest," but in turning their gaze north from the city "we begin to see the possibilities of such romantic setting as we shall find for the stirring tales of old." Collingwood, an accomplished artist and writer, produced hundreds of watercolors and sketches during his 1897 journey in Iceland, some of which he included in their wonderful book. The poet Auden writes in *Letters from Iceland*, coauthored with MacNeice, that his three months in Iceland were "among the happiest in a life, which has, so far, been unusually happy." Bill Clinton, during his stop in Iceland, sampled an Icelandic hot dog and visited Þingvellir National Park. And as for the journey of Beyoncé and Jay-Z, a writer at totaliceland.com identifying himself as Albert reports that they saw little more than the inside of a posh cabin and the one-dimensional views from a helicopter that may only be had by the ultraprivileged. "The superstars did not get but the tiniest sample of the beauty of this place," Albert writes. "For such superficial shit please turn elsewhere."[1]

I flew in earlier that morning ahead of my traveling mate, Scott Dewing, who was scheduled to arrive later that night. Scott and I have been friends since age fifteen, long enough to call each other brother, and we have made a good many journeys together. Despite the fact that Auden claims in his book that "there are very few places in Iceland where it is pleasant to walk," our plan was to get around the country on foot, from Reykjavík to Reykjavík, moving clockwise around the great Ring Road that circles the island. We would travel to various points by bus and then launch into the backcountry for a few days as we were moved to do. We might also get from here to there on foot if the way was scenic and pleasant and not particularly noisy with traffic. We had heard hitchhiking was still a thing, and we wondered how we might do with that. But mostly we came to walk, as we had both arrived at the understanding that walking is a meditative and poetic practice essential to human health and happiness. It is while walking that the mind is most free to wander and to muse and dream, and so by walking we could find relief, if only temporarily, from the trappings and stickiness of modern life. You walk not to be known but to become unknown, to disappear in a world that is so much bigger than you are.

Walking, Scott and I agreed, is also the best way to see a country. Walking asks that you make do with what little you can carry, that you slow down and make time for anything and everything and nothing at all. While walking, you travel at the pace the human body evolved to travel, reading the landscape as you go, taking in the fragrances and views and sounds that are inaccessible while traveling by train, plane, or automobile. Walking with a steady and sure gait, you notice all the details and wonders and objects along your way. You are guided by chance encounters, mishaps, surprises colored by expectations, and you are subject to all kinds of weather. Walking strips away physical and emotional comforts. You feel the ground beneath your feet and the air across your cheek, and you thirst and hunger and want, ready to encounter the world as it is. "To see things as they are makes you free," says the travel writer Paul Theroux.[2] And because walking is so physical, so visceral, you feel good in the body as you walk, and by training your body you train your mind and spirit. The walking never gets easier, but you get better. If you go walking, Scott and I had come to understand, your life becomes an adventure.

Our reasons for coming to Iceland also centered on a mutual love for learning, for mountains and rivers and fresh air, for places unencumbered by crowds and traffic and noise. What a fascinating place Iceland is. The world's oldest parliament (founded in AD 930), the world's first democratically elected female president, Vigdís Finnbogadóttir (from 1980 to 1996), one of the world's highest literacy rates (99 percent), and glaciers, volcanoes, free and clean running rivers, all of it surrounded by the rich and wild North Atlantic. These are precisely the reasons people want to travel here, and precisely the reasons no one should, for it is difficult not to argue that human beings congregating in great numbers effect great change, and not usually for the better.

With Danish roots on my mom's side (surely I am a descendant of Beowulf), I had long been curious about Denmark and Scandinavian cultures generally, and I had developed a growing love for Iceland and its sagas, which writer Jane Smiley has called "a great world treasure." Like Collingwood and Stefánsson before us, Scott and I planned to seek out sites where events in the sagas unfolded, and to learn more about how these enduringly old manuscripts were written and then preserved over time. Another aspect of our journey was to exercise and engage with the masculine qualities prized by Vikings: strength, agility, honor, loyalty, valor, daring, and courage alongside a love for poetry and storytelling, both gifts from the wandering god Óðinn. These were qualities Scott and I had long valued too, and we wondered if learning more about Vikingage Iceland would teach us something about ourselves. We didn't expect to find these qualities solely in the people of Iceland, but in Iceland itself, in its wild and rugged landscape. Perhaps we'd learn something about what we wanted to know by walking backcountry trails through the landscape familiar to the men who lived and traveled there a thousand years ago. Perhaps we'd learn something by walking through fields of summer wildflowers and grasses, by walking over black lava stretching for miles, by walking up into the jagged high peaks laced in misty snowfields, and by encounters with marine birds and arctic foxes, seals and whales offshore, and the ghosts of polar bears, an interloper that occasionally drifted in on pack ice from Greenland.

Many of these thoughts came later, after the journey. I didn't always know why I wanted to travel in Iceland before I traveled there. "You need to get to a place to discover that thing you're looking for," Theroux says. Yet one reason for going was clear for Scott and me long before our journey got off the ground. We planned this trip simply to hang out together, to reaffirm our brotherhood through shared experience, to deepen our lifelong friendship. During our walks, we would share the goings-on in our lives, express what we thought about this and that, make plans for future journeys, and share a few dirty jokes. We wanted to sample the beer and the Brennivín, the lamb and the fish soup, maybe the night life—all the things that drive much of human yearning and ambition. "It doesn't really matter where we go or what we do," Scott had said when we were planning this journey. "What matters is that we go together."

And here I was in Iceland now, awaiting Scott's arrival. I had the whole day to myself, and what would I do with it but walk, set out on foot for a look around, wander the wet streets in the rain. As much as I value good company, I also love being alone, and sometimes I prefer it. Long periods of time alone become heightened experiences in my memory. It's not that I don't get lonely—I do—but I know that loneliness helps awaken me to my surroundings and open me to people I might learn from along the way. I see and touch and taste and listen ever more clearly and intensely when I am alone. When I am alone, I am a more patient and eager observer. When I am alone, I pay attention.

What matters is that we go together.

I had already checked in to my rented room in Reykjavík, and before I wandered any farther, I needed a coffee. It was 9:47 a.m. I found Ingólfur Square, named after now-you-know-who, and just down the street a clean, well-lighted place called the Laundromat Café. There I was met with a street sign that read: "Go ahead and breastfeed. We like both babies and boobs." Though I preferred one over the other, I still felt welcomed, and so I opened the door and went in.

Inside, I came upon another sign: "Please take a seat. We will find you." I took a table in the back corner near a map of Denmark on the wall.

The main bar was an island, out of which came various waitresses who smelled like coffee and pastries. High stools lined three sides of the bar, and beneath it, books on shelves at the knees sorted by the color of their spines. Like Iceland itself, this was a literary place. The seat cushions and chairs were done up in bright red vinyl, and the hanging lamps were red too. In the basement, there was an actual laundromat, a great value to any traveler.

In case you didn't know, the original meaning of the English word "bar" is a high counter you stand at to have a drink, so named for the foot rail that ran the counter's length near the floor. Eventually stools were added so patrons might sit to drink. Soon any establishment with a bar became known as a bar. In Iceland, most bars honor a dual purpose: they are coffee shops by day and drinking establishments by night, and many, like this one, serve excellent food. I mention this for two reasons: travel is a kind of idleness by which the mind is privileged to wander, as mine was doing now; and the Laundromat Café became a kind of home in Reykjavík for Scott and me at the start and end of our journey. We took our coffee there in the mornings and dined and drank beer there into the evenings. It was the place we came to catch up on our trip notes and, yes, to wash our clothes.

A waitress did find me in that back corner and glowed in her smile as if bringing it up from the heart.

"What will you have?" she asked.

"Cappuccino," I said, which I hardly ever order. "And may I have the Wi-Fi password?"

"I love you," she said.

"What was that?"

"I love you," she said. She scanned me with her blue eyes. "I love you. That's the password. No caps or spaces."

"Of course it is," I said.

"It seems to make people happy."

"Of course it does," I said.

She told me her name, but I have since forgotten it, and I gave her mine. Later at Tapas Barinn, where Scott and I dined on puffin, we would meet a waitress who introduced herself as Saga—"It means story," she said—and I retroactively came to think of the Laundromat waitress as Saga.

"And may I have the Wi-Fi password?" I asked. "I love you," she said.

After my cappuccino, I left the café to have a look at the bay waters in the morning, the same waters where Arnarson's pillars washed ashore. I made my way to the public walk along the water and came to the impressive Harpa concert hall and conference center, a massive cubically shaped building of long, lean lines and mostly made of glass. Later I would attend a reading in this building by Icelandic novelist Auður Ava Ólafsdóttir. When she was asked what it was like being an Icelandic writer, she answered: "Oh, constant disruption—working in a marginal language, bankruptcy, and volcanoes." I messed around in the rain for a good half hour looking at stuff and generally feeling self-important. The runners and walkers were out, making haste along the waterfront, and I decided to move on too, picking up a good rhythm, walking fast and sure as the rain slowed and stopped and the sun came out. Up ahead, a small group of people were gathered around some kind of massive sculpture or monument.

I soon arrived at the *Sun Voyager*, by Jón Gunnar Árnason, a stainless-steel sculpture of a Viking ship, a blue-water boat shiny in the sun with a tridentlike bow and stern and trident-headed sailors positioned along the keel line. The sculpture seemed alive, and I thought I could feel the ship's keel plunging and shaking in the sea, skimming the foamy waves and the green sheets of water, the sails running on stiff winds, heaving ever onward, the prow loping over the sea's currents on the hunt. As such, I felt the way such vessels call to men, inviting a journey into the unknown. I could not help but think of Arnarson, who boarded a ship and sailed into unmapped waters, never to return.[3] Standing where his pillars washed ashore, I concluded that what Arnarson was after on his journey was not just a new country, but a new self. A traveler who pushes off into dark and stormy seas keeps a quiet understanding that somewhere in the world there may be a self better suited to him than the one he has at home, and that self rises easily from a new place better suited to it. Such a traveler asks, if only unconsciously, *Who will I become where I am going that suits me better than who I am now?*

From where I stood near the *Sun Voyager* positioned on the bay water, I decided to seek a higher viewpoint, a vantage from which to see Reykjavík and to get a better sense of the place. I made my slow way south across the city, a straight shot down Frakkastígur street and up the hill to the shining tower of Hallgrímskirkja. It was comely, this church, the white tower climbing into the sky and shadowing a statue of Icelander Leifr Eiricsson (AD 940-1020), the supposed first European to land in North America in about AD 1000, possibly at L'Anse aux Meadows, Newfoundland, a site I would explore a few years after my time in Iceland.

Looking out from Hallgrímskirkja on the hill, a hill Arnarson surely climbed before there was a church or even a city here, I surveyed the mountains and waters extending into the sea. A flurry of thoughts raced through me. Travel, as I experience it, is mechanical and messy and tedious and tiresome, a disruption to your familiar diet and healthful sleep. It causes night sweats and bad dreams, constipation and aches in the bones and joints, a wearing thin of your patience, long periods of waiting for this or that to happen, and all manner of other discomforts. Travel is a full schedule of making schedules in order to do something you must make more schedules for. It can be adventurous, but gone are the days of traveling to an undiscovered country, to far-off exotic and impenetrable lands. In the twenty-first century, with a world population exceeding eight billion and reasonably cheap airfare, it seems everyone is going everywhere all the time. The places you would think to travel have already been overtraveled, and more travelers mean more government regulation and boundaries and the herding of tourists down various tourist trails that lead almost exclusively to trinket shops, restaurants, and hotels. Everyone sees the same thing, most through the back of a smartphone. And then, of course, it is difficult not to consider the environmental impact of travel, the unavoidable great carbon cost to the future every time you step out your door. I wondered why I bother to travel at all.

One way for me to make sense of what I'm doing is to write about it. While Iceland would not be a journey into the unknown, the time I spent later at my writing desk would be, the surface of it covered with the pages of my notes and me laboring to bring a story alive to the page. "And again the writer / Runs howling to his art," writes Auden in his

I could feel
the ship's keel
plunging and
shaking in the sea.

poem "Journey to Iceland." To write about the journey is to reach back through time to relive what I did and saw in a place, what I experienced and felt, so that I may recover the people and the moments I will one day forget. Surprises come when revisiting the past this way, whether distant or recent, when reacquiring a past I thought I had left behind. I stumble onto a delightful sense of renewal, certainty, and belonging. Yet writing always includes the risk of remembering what I wanted to forget. Even as it is impossible to become who I once was, it can sometimes be impossible to forget what I have newly remembered. It would be easier to stay safely at home, of course, not to travel and then not to write, but because the world will not come to me, I must go to it. And going to it, the great task is to see. To see clearly and objectively and to understand what is going on in a place and why it is important to know it. The shield or barrier to seeing clearly is most often fear and loneliness. How does one face fear and loneliness while traveling? Can they be mastered, and if not, how can they be managed? The best way I have found to overcome my own resistance to the discomforts of travel is to go with a friend and then to write about it, and when I do, it is best not to strive or push too hard. It is best to let the journey map itself.

I stood on that high hill before Hallgrímskirkja watching the play of light across the city and on the surface of the surrounding waters. I sensed a clarity in the sky that penetrated everything and distorted it too, like looking through the prism of a diamond. Perhaps now I understood what Lord Dufferin meant when he wrote that in Reykjavík "the effects of light and shadow are the purest [he] ever saw." I stood long in that moment, letting it stretch out, and the rest of the day I wandered in Reykjavík, through the streets and parks and in and out of shops, the rain coming on and going away and the sun illuminating my steps. In a city so close to the Arctic Circle in summer, it was nearly impossible to judge time by the sun. Evening came easily and quietly, and I soon realized that Scott had already landed out at Keflavík and had possibly traveled into town to our rented room. I turned my steps unhurriedly in that direction.

When I arrived and opened the door to the room, there he was stretched out on one of the two beds, the unshaven, hulking form of him, his bald head against a pillow, his eyes closed as if in slumber. He hardly stirred and did not bother to get up.

"What took you so long, Caswell?" he said. "I need a pint of something and some food."

"You're in luck," I said. "I happen to know a good laundromat just around the corner."

Walking to Laxness

REYKJAVÍK TO MOSFELLSBÆR, AND AROUND

Halldór Laxness, Iceland's only Nobel laureate (for literature, in 1955), lived most of his later years in a modest house near Mosfellsbær on the road Þingvallavegur, northeast of Reykjavík. If you keep going on that road, it leads eventually to Þingvellir National Park, home to the famed Law Rock where the Vikings established the world's first democratic republic in AD 930. If you had to choose a quiet place to write in the midst of Iceland's past, present, and future, this was it. I had read Laxness's novel *Independent People*, and the short biography printed inside that book proclaims him "the undisputed master of contemporary Icelandic fiction," not to be outdone by the fact that the International Astronomical Union named a crater on Mercury after him. So it made a lot of sense to offer him a day of my time by making a visit to his house, opened to the public in 2004.

Studying our map, Scott and I determined that we might walk to the Laxness house from Hótel Laxnes in Mosfellsbær, where we were staying, along a footpath that would keep us off the main road and away from the rush of speeding cars. On our way out of the hotel, the friendly concierge asked what we had planned for our day, and we told him.

"Honestly, guys," he said, "it's not worth it. It's a house with a bunch of books."

"We'll have a look anyway," I said.

"And we're going to walk it," Scott said.

"Walk it? Do you know how far it is from here? About ten kilometers," the fellow said.

"Eight," I said. "One way."

He gave us a pained look. "You must really like this writer."

"Don't you?" I asked.

He looked at us blankly. "Not at all," he said.

The day was a mix of sun and cloud, a blue sky day, bluer than the eyes of Saga, or Björk, which are really more brown with green overtones, but who can really say from her photographs and video, all the black and white, the fantastical costumes, the nipple piercings, her mesmeric voice, but the point is that the sky was blue and fluffy with clouds, fast-moving in dramatic pushes, like a pulsing beacon on a hill. It had been raining (which is often the case in Iceland), and when you are in Iceland and only eight kilometers from the Laxness house, you go.[4] You go despite the fact that the concierge at a hotel named after the great man just told you it wasn't worth it, just told you, in so many words, that he can think of nothing so excruciating as to read a Laxness novel, except maybe to walk eight kilometers to his house. For travelers like us, it matters very little whether it is worth it or not. You can only determine value after you have done a thing, not before, notwithstanding whether another's judgment is circumspect, especially if that judgment is passed by a local about his own place. Even if a thing is not worth doing, doing it is usually better than sitting at home or in a hotel and not doing it. Of course we would do it, and we would walk. We would walk to get the soreness out of our legs, to feel that cool northern air on our faces, and see some bright new country.

The soreness got into our legs when we walked to Mosfellsbær from Reykjavík the day before, first through the center of the city, then out across the neighborhoods, passing the Icelandic Phallological Museum—"We'll have a look when we come back around to Reykjavík," I reassured Scott—and heading down into the green ditch along the rushing

Icelandic horses nuzzling our fingers.

freeway, then onto a back road where the green countryside rolled out before us, Icelandic horses nuzzling our fingers along the fence line, quiet farmhouses overlooking verdant pasturage, and two mountains to our east, Hafrafell and Reykjafell, easy sentinels that guarded us along the way. All told, it turned out to be a twenty-six-kilometer day. It completely wrecked us, as it was our first real walk of the trip, and we were packed too heavy, especially me, and sadly out of shape.

I've backpacked a lot, and I know better, but for some reason, before I left home I could not stop putting stuff in my pack. I carried the essentials required for a walking tour of Iceland: sleeping bag, tent, stove, cook gear, my clothes, first aid kit. I carried my iPhone, a Garmin GPS, an eleven-inch MacBook Air inside a Pelican case, a ceramic water purifier in a country with the cleanest water on earth, and four copies of my own books, gifts, I thought, for wonderful people we might meet along the way.[5] I normally wouldn't have carried so much tech—just a pen and notebook was my habit—but I imagined myself holed up in a seaside hotel for a few weeks after Scott flew home, a long view of the blue waters out a window with a mountain headland towering along a peninsula, tapping out beautiful prose; that never happened. Walking the roads, I could justify the phone and GPS, but the laptop? It was a luxury I appreciated when we got into a room, but on foot it was an annoying burden.

At the end of our walk to Mosfellsbær the day before, we dragged into the town campsite, set up, and cooked a hurried meal as the sky darkened with black clouds. An old man walked by our camp, smiled, and said, "It will be a big storm tonight." And it was. I slept fitfully and woke at dawn to a toothed wind trying to uproot our tent. In a fit, we broke camp in the storm and retreated to a tiny shelter behind the campground's toilet, made coffee in the misty wind, and walked through the rain to Hótel Laxnes, willing to pay nearly anything for a room and a hot shower. That is how we found ourselves talking to this young fellow at the desk, who took umbrage with our homage to Laxness and our happy plan to walk the road to the Laxness house.

Carrying only a little water, some light snacks, and our essential documents, we made our way through town and out the paved walking path with green trees planted all in a row. We came along what seemed to be a preschool or perhaps a day care where children played outside in the after-wet of the heavy rain. A cluster of them moved off as we came by, leaving a lone boy with thick glasses and prominent front teeth blocking our path. He appeared to be stunned, like a bird that has just hit a window, his neck bent up, his eyes like a pair of big binoculars. We must have looked like beings from an alien planet. I could not help but pause to ask him a question, which I sort of knew the answer to already.

"Does this paved walking path go a long way?" I said. "We'd like to avoid walking on the main road."

He blinked, and blinked again, sizing us up. "It goes a werry long way," he said. "You should take a car."

Born in 1902 on the farm across the road from the house where we were headed, the writer Halldór Laxness lived a long and productive life, with thirteen major novels, five plays, a number of memoirs, and numerous collections of short stories and essays to his credit—sixty-two books in sixty-eight years—and his work has been translated into forty-three languages. He admired Hemingway and translated two of his books into Icelandic, *A Farewell to Arms* (1941) and *A Moveable Feast* (1966). Like Hemingway, he preferred to write standing up. After he won the Nobel Prize, Laxness became a noted socialite, welcoming dignitaries and royals in his modest home. On Sundays he hosted music concerts, a tradition that has continued during summer months since his death in 1998. Music, Laxness maintained, is superior to language in expressing the range of feelings human beings experience in communion with the cosmos. He noted that Bach was the best of the best, and he often played Bach's music himself on his Steinway grand. When asked what book he would take to a desert island, Laxness cheated the question by answering *The Well-Tempered Clavier*, Bach's collection of solo keyboard music written to instruct young musicians.[6] Laxness loved the finer things in life and collected cool furniture: his beloved butterfly chair, for example, and a low-slung calfskin chair that apparently only he was allowed to sit in. The walls of his house are covered in paintings, many made by his friends, several of them portraits of him. He sported about the countryside and into town in his favorite car, a 1968 silver Jaguar, still parked outside his home (winning the Nobel includes a generous cash prize), and it was this Jaguar that greeted Scott and me as we ambled up the driveway to the front door.

Pausing in front of the house, I took in the views. A squarish white, two-story home with a relatively flat roof, a garden, and modest pool that Laxness's daughter, who lives nearby, still swims in after museum hours. The house sits off the highway against a hill in a rugged drainage, the river Kaldakvísl, which teems with arctic char, and which Laxness frequently walked up with his dog. In a photograph of one such walk, you can see his trusty dog, white like the house, trotting along the river's edge while the man himself, wearing a woolen suit and cap, walks *in* the river, the frigid waters covering his leather shoes and soaking his pants.

It is an odd feeling to tour the home of a man who is dead, to gaze on the things he collected and owned and that surrounded him in his daily life. I wondered if Laxness's things defined him in such a way that something of the spirit of the man still resided in them. And I wondered if our visit honored Laxness, or was it rather a nosy or even voyeuristic curiosity that pushed up hard against the morbid. I don't know, but the place did not feel like the house of a man long dead, but rather the house of a man who had stepped out for a pint of fresh milk and would be returning within the hour. As Scott and I were the only ones there, I felt like an invitee and half expected to be greeted at the door by Auður, Laxness's wife, awaiting us for tea. Instead, we were met by a caretaker who offered an audio guide in English, which we accepted.

At the entrance, we were introduced to Laxness's grandfather clock and the staircase winding up to his study. I am fascinated by writers' studies, and this one was unremarkable in most every way: a few pictures on the wall, a wall of books, a chair for resting, and the desk and chair where he wrote. The curtains looked like those of any middle-class 1950s family, stiff and drab.

Perhaps the casual observer might see in Laxness himself that same stiff drabness. He was clean-shaven, except for a sometimes mustache looking not unlike that of a prominent German madman of the day; a military-style haircut over a balding head; and a sturdy chin that became more prominent as he aged. But his politics were anything but drab. Laxness was born a Catholic then converted to Marxism, a new kind of religion that capitalists associated with Satan (I suppose many still do). Later, watching Stalin fall prey to corruption, he renounced Marxism, along with all dogma. If Laxness believed in anything in his later years, he believed in literature and music, the *Tao Te Ching* and nature, and in his companion dogs. "Come what may and go what may," Laxness writes in *Independent People*, "a man always has the memories of his dogs"; "a dog is the only animal that understands a man"; and "whatever a man

The river Kaldakvísl, which Laxness frequently walked up with his dog.

seeks he will find—in his dog." He loved coffee: "Presently, the smell of coffee began to fill the room. This was morning's hallowed moment. In such a fragrance the perversity of the world is forgotten and the soul is inspired with faith in the future." And he loved travel and wild places: "Nothing nurtures the poet's gift so much as solitude on long mountain journeys."

This novel, *Independent People*—beloved by the American writer Annie Proulx, less beloved by Auden, who writes in *Letters from Iceland* that Laxness "makes the farmers more unpleasant than they really are"—may be Laxness's masterpiece. It's the story of the common Icelandic man, Bjartur of Summerhouses, who struggles in the harsh climate of Iceland to save enough money to buy his own farm, and so become independent. "I say for my part," Bjartur says, "that a man lives in vain until he is independent. People who aren't independent aren't people. A man who isn't his own master is as bad as a man without a dog." Laxness claimed he worked his whole life to promote the "hidden people," not the huldufólk (elves, trolls, and whatnot) that travelers to Iceland hear so much about, but the proletariat who are beaten down by the wealthy and powerful. "The love of freedom and independence has always been a characteristic of the Icelandic people," Laxness writes. Many Americans will identify with Icelanders on this point, and who knows, perhaps a love for freedom and independence came to North America from Iceland. After all, the Icelander Leifr Eiricsson made landfall in North America centuries before Columbus sailed west, and before the Declaration of Independence. America, according to Laxness, is a place where "a man can be anything he likes."

After our visit to the Laxness house, Scott and I stepped back onto the road to Mosfellsbær, walking evenly and efficiently between the low mountains while sifting clouds held onto their rain, and the sun came in on its summer arc: the brightness of Iceland. We arrived at the hotel tired and spent but jazzed by our good day, only to be shuttled into the dining room by a new fellow at the front desk who, unlike the other fellow, seemed to have held on to his youthful optimism. "Take a seat, gentlemen," he said. "We have a special menu tonight." We ordered Guinness, and quite suddenly two plates of the special menu arrived: three massive pieces of fried chicken, a mound of mashed potatoes as tall as Devil's Tower, a side of boiled vegetables, and an unlimited supply of brown bread. It was glorious. So glorious.

After we had our fill, we retired to the bar, where a group of local men had taken up their usual posts. They raised their glasses to us as we sat down. On the big screen at the back of the room they had settled on an American movie for the evening, *The Rock* (1996), with Nicolas Cage and Sean Connery playing the good guys and Ed Harris playing the bad guy, though in the movie who is good and who is bad vacillates back and forth. Harris's character is a US marine brigadier general who positions himself against his government because it treats soldiers as expendable (read the proletariat), and Connery's character is a British SAS captain gone criminal who is forced into service by the US government to take down Harris's character (read the proletariat used by the government to combat the proletariat). Cage plays an FBI agent who comes to question who and what is good and bad. Laxness would have loved this movie.

Scott and I settled in with fresh pints of Guinness to watch and drink with these Icelandic men, these local boys, who'd come in from work to pour off the day's stresses. We cheered when they cheered, laughed when they laughed, and urged our movie heroes on. And then, in a quiet moment while our heroes negotiated the sewers beneath Alcatraz, Nicolas Cage tells Sean Connery that he will "do his best." Connery responds: "Losers are always whining about their best; winners go home and fuck the prom queen."

The Icelanders looked over at us. We looked over at the Icelanders. And the house came down in laughter. And that, my friends, is how you discover common cause between two free and independent nations.

On Not Looking into Snorri's Pool

FROM MOSFELLSBÆR TO BORGARNES AND REYKHOLT

U p Highway 1 out of Reykjavík, east and north past Mount Esja at Mosfellsbær, across Hvalfjörður by a tunnel going under it, you come to Borgarnes, where Scott and I rented a car for the day and drove east toward the interior on Highway 50 to Reykholt.[7] That road follows the river Reykjadalsá above its confluence with the Hvítá, the white river, named for its milky waters, which flow from the second largest glacier in Iceland, Langjökull. Reykholt is situated in a quiet, fertile valley— Collingwood and Stefánsson describe it as a town "on a little hill rising in the midst of flat meadows"—between barren lava fields on the north and the ramparts of the glacial plateau on the south. I wanted to have a look at Snorri's pool, a small, stone-lined hot spring pool where Snorri Sturluson (1179-1241), one of Iceland's great chieftains, soaked his bones.

Scott and I parked and got out at Snorrastofa, the modern medieval study center celebrating Sturluson's life and work that stands tall and stately like a great white massif. It was a glorious summer day near the Arctic Circle, with highs in the mid-sixties, light winds, partly cloudy with lovely rays of light coming through. The valley is as green as England this time of year, and farther up the hill is Reykholt Forest, a few hectares of planted conifers (dwarf mountain and bristlecone pine, Russian larch and Norway spruce), an attempt at restoring a little piece of ground to conditions before the settlement of Iceland.

A small, stone-lined hot spring pool where Snorri Sturluson soaked his bones.

Snorri Sturluson lived during a literary golden age marked by Iceland's transition from oral to written culture. He was a poet and scholar, a wealthy landowner, a politician, a husband and father, a traveler and philanderer. He was susceptible to the charms of beautiful women, though women were unlikely to have been susceptible to him but for his status and wealth—images of Sturluson recall Santa Claus, a face capable of strong emotion and the promise of delicate sentiment. When trouble came his way, he usually opted for diplomacy, and yet he still got crosswise with his onetime ally, King Haakon IV of Norway, and was murdered in his cellar not far from his famed pool. He wrote, among other things, two of the great books of his age, the *Prose Edda*, a guidebook for young poets and a sourcebook for much of what we now know as Norse mythology, and the *Heimskringla*, a history of the kings of Norway. Sturluson, and others before and after him, helped lift Iceland out of obscurity and transform it into one of the most literate and well-read nations in the world. Iceland is a nation of the book, a nation of storytellers, of readers and writers. Writers are loved and respected here, which explains why there are so many of them. One in ten of Iceland's 330,000 people, the BBC has reported, will likely publish a book.

"What's so great about Snorri?" Scott said, as we made our way across the gravel parking lot.

"Oh, I don't know," I said. "He's one of the greatest figures of medieval Europe. A wealthy landowner. Wrote books that transformed a nation. He's kinda like Iceland's Homer."

"Snorri," Scott said. "Snoooorrrriii. Oh, look. There's his statue. Have to get your photo with Snorri."

"Yeah, great," I said, posing beneath the towering figure.

"And you say he's got a pool around here?"

"Yeah," I said. "The stones are original. Maybe some of them were laid down by the man himself."

"Probably not," Scott said. "That shit happened a long time ago. And since he was rich, he probably had poor laborers do it for him. Or slaves. Let's go for a walk up in those trees."

In Reykholt Forest, we rose above the village on a wood-chip path to look down on the steeple of the new church, the steeple of the old church next to the cemetery, a complex of greenhouses farther off, and the green sweep of the valley leading into the mountains. A road and some fences broke the varying scene. Nothing much was happening except a little brown bird twittering on a branch and the slow unfolding of the day. We were in this place, in this moment, and the quiet and cool skies seemed an expansive roof sheltering the stories of a long-ago time. I felt obligated to look more closely.

All travel, at least for me, feels hurried and a little desperate, and in returning home from a journey I often wonder if I saw and felt deeply enough, if I learned anything new, if I had an original moment by hunting the edge of experience. I often wonder if I regarded my companions—those who traveled with me and those who stayed behind—with enough kindness and patience and grace, and with enough love. And so, in returning from a journey, I often feel a lingering anxiety that drives me to desire, above all things, to depart again. If I go again, such is my reasoning, I just might get it right.

On the way back down, we stopped at the museum. We were eerily alone except for a woman seated at the front desk.

"Is the museum open?" I asked.

"Já," the woman said, sucking in her breath. I had heard this expression a number of times now and found it somehow comforting, even encouraging.[8]

"What can we see if we go inside?"

"Exhibits," she said. "You can see exhibits, and read about Snorri Sturluson on the walls. One thousand krona for entrance."

"Do you want to go in?" I asked Scott.

"Now, you know I ain't gonna to do that," he said. "I can read about Snorri online for free. Or in a book."

"Good point," I said.

"If you're not going inside, I guess we might have a look at that pool where this dude liked to soak," he said.

Iceland converted to Christianity in AD 1000, and Sturluson was a Christian, but in his *Prose Edda* he is pagan in his heart. Part 1, "Gylfaginning," or "The Delusion of Gylfi," which the book's reputation is based on, instructs young poets through the tale of a Swedish king, Gylfi, who is deluded into believing in the Æsir, the pantheon of pagan gods, especially Óðinn, the wanderer. Gylfi disguises himself and takes on the name Gangleri, which means "the Wayworn," another name for Óðinn. He appears before the gods in Ásgarðr unaware that his true identity is already known, which only underscores his delusion. His assumed name also expresses wisdom acquired through travel, but because he lacks wisdom he is a kind of warning to all pagans who, from a Christian perspective, blindly believe in the Æsir and deny the Christian god. But the human spirit is a thing strangely put together, as Sturluson the Christian wrote a book celebrating Norse mythology and his pagan ancestors. Beyond the book's poetic instruction, I take to heart not Gylfi's delusion but the story's central wisdom, which is a pagan ideal: the created world is fragile and temporary, and one day, at the time of Ragnarök, the world will be destroyed and a new world will rise to take its place. According to the story, the temporality of the universe the gods created does not diminish the glory and beauty of its creation.

In search of Snorri's pool, Scott and I walked through the grassy field before Snorrastofa to a pond where the ground was tractored and tilled up like some great beast had been at work with its claws. I noticed a section of black pipe cast aside on the hummocky ground near the water's edge, a few deciduous trees, recently planted. We had no map or guide, but I did have an image of the pool in my mind, and this pond was not what I had imagined.

"Is this Snorri's pool?" I said dumbly.

"I don't know," Scott said.

"I know you don't know."

"Then why did you ask?"

"I wasn't asking," I said. "I was commenting."

"Sounded like you were asking to me," Scott said.

"This can't be it."

"So, where the hell is the pool?" Scott said. "Looks like a bomb went off around here."

We wandered near the eastern edge of the field where we discovered a few geothermic vents, one with a section of broken precast concrete pipe sticking upright out of the ground. It was filled with weird bubbling water, and sitting inside it, like a stirring spoon in a pot of soup, an old rib bone, probably from a cow or maybe a horse. A shiver ran over me from the wind. Perhaps a great troll was at work here, tearing up the ground in its rage, killing horses and eating horsemeat in the night.

Collingwood and Stefánsson claim that Snorri's pool had "recently been cleared of its ruin, and one may bathe in it as Snorri did." This didn't look like a pool anyone would dare bathe in, but of course Collingwood and Stefánsson visited in 1897. Perhaps there have been some changes since then? Scott and I looked at each other and shrugged, and with the

Perhaps a troll was at work here, killing horses and eating horsemeat in the night.

glee of travelers who shake off the dust of one stage before hurrying forth upon another, we snapped a few photos, walked to the car, and drove up the road to Húsafell.

What had we come all this way to see, I asked privately of myself, if not to see Snorri's pool, and now driving along this winding valley road, I concluded that we had not seen it, but some other strange water, the merit of which remained to be realized. I wanted to feel what the poet Keats felt when he looked into Chapman's Homer: the opening of a new world so delicious that it kept him up all night foraging and tasting and dribbling over the words of the master, which inspired him to compose the most heralded of his early sonnets.[9] I wanted to learn, as Keats had learned in reading Homer, that Snorri, Iceland's poet of poets, was a gateway to some fantastic new realm, and perhaps looking into that pool, looking into the dark waters bubbling up from the center of the earth, would lead me there.

In Húsafell, we walked a trail up Bæjargil, a narrow gorge of razorlike rock that a glacial stream flowed through. Along the way we paused to admire stone faces carved into the rock by local artist Páll Guðmundsson: a woman's face and her beehive hair, a wild man with a bird at his shoulder (possibly an image of Óðinn), a Roman-nosed face with vacuous eyes. The sky grayed and foretold rain, and when rain came, the rock went black and slick, writ in water like the surface of an alien planet where patches of white and purple flowers were all that returned us to the earth. I felt that I was climbing up the canyon to shake off a lesser part of myself, and as the rain fell and wetted my head, all my sins were forgiven. I noted, in that variegated moment, the slow-paced way of every journey, the slow-paced grind of every life and how it is possible to look into a distant past and condense that long time into a brief and beautiful story, to taste it in all its elevation and energy, to bring it back to the center. Here, in the cold wet canyon of Bæjargil, I felt free to wander, free to hope, and free to love whatever or whoever happened upon my way.

We ambled farther on, farther up, now walking along the frontier of hope, and discovered a series of cloven hoofprints in a spot of mud along a pile of rounded droppings. A ewe? A goat? A faun? The rain fell on as we reached a high cliff, and coming over it, falling in long tracks of lovely lines, the soft waters of the glacial stream. This was the end, the very limit of the canyon, and it was here that the stony skeleton of the world was vigorously displayed. We turned and made our way down in a hail of sunshine.

Back in Borgarnes, we traded our clothes for our swim trunks at the town pool and dropped into the clear geothermal waters for a soak. As we let those waters wash us out, let our muscles and bones drain of all troubles and considerations, I realized I had been seeking an adventure all my life, a pure dispassionate adventure such as befell early and heroic voyagers. To be in Iceland with my old friend, to have seen what we had seen, was to find my dream realized. Ending a day like this, I thought, made all our next days possible.

Along the way we paused to admire stone faces
carved into the rock.

Eating the Pylsur of Heaven, Part One
FROM BORGARNES TO STYKKISHÓLMUR

First we eat, then we do everything else.
— M. F. K. Fisher

To get to the Westfjords—one of the wildest and most beautiful regions in Iceland—Scott and I would take the sea route, a smooth and easy passage across Breiðafjörður (Broad Fjord), with views of Snæfellsnes and its great glacier, Snæfellsjökull, the famed setting of Jules Verne's *Journey to the Center of the Earth*. Breiðafjörður is jam-packed with tiny islands, uncountable according to local legend (but nothing really is uncountable), and the ferry stops at one of them, Flatey, where you can camp or rent a room for the night. As Scott and I were headed into the Hornstrandir, the most northerly and remote peninsula of the northerly and remote Westfjords, we made our innocent way to the port town of Stykkishólmur, where, little did we know, we would break our virgin knot eating the best wieners in all the world.

Iceland is known for its hot dogs, or pylsur, as they are called. How could we resist when we passed a hot dog stand on the left as we were walking the road into town from our campsite? If you want to get technical, the hot dog stand that tourists talk about is in Reykjavík, Bæjarins Beztu Pylsur (translation: "The Best Hot Dog in Town"). Its fame has traveled far and beyond, as it was voted the best hot dog in Europe. Before that, Bill Clinton gave it a try on his 2004 visit to Iceland, ordering a hot dog with brown mustard only, so plain and laughable by Icelandic standards that they made "Clinton style" part of their menu. It is said that Madonna, too, snacked on a wiener here, and a member of the band Metallica. A line snakes out from the window of this red kiosk near the waterfront, pretty much always, even at two a.m.

But that place is that place. The place Scott and I were going to in Stykkishólmur—Meistarapylsur, or "Master Sausages"—is a bit farther off the tourist way, perhaps little known, with no long wait. A better place altogether, at least by my standards.

We walked right up to read the menu and felt the surprising heat and glory of a ray of light emanating from the serving window, haloing the young woman slinging dogs. Leaning out to look us in the eyes, her long darkened hair falling torrentlike over her shoulders, she didn't speak but rather offered a kind of hot dog telepathy to invite our order.

"I'll have the Jóakim," Scott said, so sure of himself that it made me feel small.

The Jóakim, no ordinary hot dog, was "a deep-fried hot dog," the menu told us, "with cheese sauce, salsa sauce and Doritos chips, melted cheese and spice." And when you read "Doritos chips," dear American, do not think Scott would be handed one of those little bags packaged for school lunches. No. The chips are hand-broken into small pieces and spread across the landscape of the saucy bun, giving every bite a delicate crunch.

Next, it was my turn to order, and I ordered the 14-2.

The 14-2 was not an ordinary dog either but a "hot dog grilled in a special way. With baked beans, sauces, melted cheese, and spice." The special way the dog was to be grilled was yet unclear, but I knew I had to have it grilled that way all the same.

At this, the young woman at the window smiled. "Would you like the baked beans on that?" she asked.

"Yes, I would," I said.

"The 14-2 was my second choice," Scott said.

"Would you like the baked beans on that?" she asked.

Iceland, like every region of the world, has plenty more adventures in food. Beyond the hot dog, try puffin, that cute marine bird, often served smoked and arranged on your plate in a stack of purply lumps. Later Scott and I would try puffin in a blueberry Brennivín sauce, Brennivín being that famed Icelandic spirit also known as Black Death. Skyr, a thousand-year-old Icelandic favorite, is a cultured milk dish not unlike yogurt. First you remove the cream to make butter. With the remaining skim milk, you remove the whey to make skyr. The whey may then be used to culture fresh milk or drunk as is. Nothing is wasted. Minke whale is still available on restaurant menus, accompanied by canvassers on the street calling for a ban on hunting and eating whale. But Iceland is mostly famous for its fish, an island nation graced by the world-class fishery of the North Atlantic. Fish soup is a restaurant standard, and a big bowl with hearty bread is inexpensive and satisfying. Harðfiskur, or wind-dried haddock, a fish jerky eaten with butter, is available everywhere as an anytime snack. Cod cheeks sautéed in butter, or beer-battered and fried, are fabulous. And the fish dish every traveler hears about but wants to avoid is hákarl, or putrefied shark meat. Basking shark is the preferred species, the second largest fish in the world,[10] a slow-moving and generally unaggressive beast, killed and buried underground then exhumed and hung in an old barn for months until it rots into a white, chunky, cheeselike goo. I did not try it but read that it tastes of ammonia; one traveler remarked that it is like eating "the gangrenous, blackened toes of a long-dead polar explorer which have been defrosted and left behind a radiator for a few days."[11] Hákarl is primarily made at Bjarnarhöfn, a farm on Snæfellsnes that dates back to Iceland's settlement period, not far from where Scott and I were now.

At the hot dog stand in Stykkishólmur, the warm sun falling over us, we took up a seat at the outdoor table and, without ceremony, tucked right in. For me, the experience was mostly a distortion of zip and whirr, so measureless as to nearly escape description. What vividly returns to my memory is the loud snap at the teeth, so crisp and tight was that wiener, and then a taste explosion ominously beautiful, the beans and spice coming together so completely the sense aches at it.

One difference between an Icelandic hot dog and the dogs from everywhere else is that instead of a combination of beef and pork, you get beef and pork *and* lamb—and Icelandic lamb, Icelanders boast, is unrivaled by any on earth. "You see, the lambs of Iceland are free to roam where they please," Scott and I were told later by a woman who gave us a ride. "They can eat the grass on the hills, or the seaweed by the sea, at their pleasure. They are free and independent. This is why they are the best in the world."

The hot dog went down far too rapidly, and for a moment I felt like Joey Chestnut, who holds the world's record in hot dog eating, seventy-five with buns in ten minutes.[12] I wanted another and another, but I lifted my eyes to the blue skies, the warm sunlight returning me to my senses. Scott and I tossed away our wrappers and walked the road to the ferry terminal to arrange our passage to the Westfjords.

At the ferry terminal, two young women were working the counter, and Scott asked about the schedule for the next day. In order to catch the bus to Ísafjörður on the other side, we'd have to take the morning ferry instead of the afternoon one, but we wouldn't want to do that, we were told, because tomorrow was Sunday and the bus didn't run on Sundays from the terminal on the other side. If we took the afternoon ferry tomorrow, however, we could go halfway across the bay and stay the night on Flatey Island, and then continue early Monday morning to the terminal at Brjánslækur and catch the bus to Ísafjörður Monday afternoon. That sounded like an excellent plan, and one of the women went to work on our tickets.

"Where are you from?" she asked, typing on her keyboard.

"From the States," Scott said. "I'm from Oregon. He's from Texas."

"I live in Texas," I said, "but I'm *from* Oregon."

"An important distinction," Scott said.

"Well, I'm from Reykjavík," she said. "But I live in Stykkishólmur. Just for the summer."

"Summer job?" Scott asked.

"That's right," she said. "I'm at university. I came here for a summer job for one reason only."

"What's that?" Scott said.

"The hot dogs here are fantastic," she said. "I love them."

"You're kidding," Scott said.

"No. I'm not kidding. Here is even better than in Reykjavík."

"We just tried the hot dogs at that stand out near the grocery," I said.

"Meistarapylsur," she said. "The best. I love them so much. I can't get enough. Did you have the one with baked beans?" she asked.

"I did," I said.

"To die for."

"We'll have to go again," Scott said. "I need to try that one."

Hot dogs really are the national food, come to find out, and like so many other foods they were born of a need for preservation. Cheese and yogurt and skyr are all methods for preserving milk. Jams and jellies and pies are methods for preserving fruit. Sausages are one of the best ways to preserve meat, and making them is an ancient art. Homer (not to be confused with Hormel) mentions blood sausage in *The Odyssey*, and the *Apicius*, a fourth-century book of Roman cookery, includes a recipe for smoked sausage. Preserving meat this way is even older still, as twenty thousand years ago Paleo peoples boiled meat, then carried and stored it in the harvested stomachs and intestines of animals. Modern sausages owe much to Germanic peoples, among the greatest sausage makers in the world. The term "frankfurter" comes from that sausage town, Frankfurt, Germany, and "wiener" from Vienna, Austria. A German immigrant brought the hot dog to America in the late nineteenth century. The origin of the term "hot dog" is hard to trace. A number of tales are circulating, many false, and one even accuses hot dog makers of using dog meat, which, in late nineteenth-century America, might have been sometimes true. "Political regimes come and go," Bruce Kraig writes in *Hot Dog: A Global History*, "but sausages remain."

After a beer or two harborside, Scott and I made our way up the hill to the Library of Water.[13] This rounded building with a bank of windows looking onto the fjord had once been a real library, but the books are gone now, replaced by a permanent installation by artist Roni Horn. Positioned throughout the space are twenty-four glass columns, each filled with water from one of Iceland's twenty-four major glaciers. All but one of the country's major glaciers are receding, and when they are gone—the unstoppable death knell of climate change—the Library of Water will be art and archive, monument and memorial. A light illuminates the columns from within, and sunlight streaming in through the windows illuminates them from without. You walk among these columns of watery light like a faun in a forest of fantastical trees. On the floor are words suggesting weather: *hot, dry, nice, destructive*. I paused at one column, curious, because the light inside seemed to be turned off. I inquired of the attendant.

"You know," she said, "the bulb in that one just went out one day. It's a smaller glacier in the interior called Okjökull. Or we just say Ok" (pronounced "ahk"). "So I called up Roni to let her know we would replace the bulb. Then we found out that of the twenty-four glaciers in Iceland, Ok is the first one to go. It's gone. Completely melted. So we decided not to replace the bulb."

In 2014 the Icelandic Meteorological Office declared the Ok glacier dead. In 2019 a ceremony was held at the glacier site that included Ice-

You walk among these columns like a faun in a forest of fantastical trees.

land's prime minister and environmental minister. The party dedicated a plaque with "a letter to the future" written in both Icelandic and English. The plaque reads:

Ok is the first Icelandic glacier to lose its status as a glacier.
In the next 200 years all our glaciers are expected to
follow the same path.
This monument is to acknowledge that we know
what is happening and what needs to be done.
Only you know if we did it.

After dinner, Scott and I made the steep but short walk to the top of Súgandisey, a basalt island approachable by land across the harbor causeway. We stood at the lighthouse overlooking Breiðafjörður and our next day's ferry route. We could see the waters shimmering off the evening polar sun and the many islands spreading out over the blue distance. The fjord, its islands, and the surrounding shoreline have been an important food-producing region since the settlement of Iceland. The fjord is rich in fish and marine mammals, as well as marine birds, and the islands and shoreline are rich in fine soils suitable for grazing and haymaking. Most of Iceland's iconic foods can be found here, and a look into the past can offer an understanding of how these foods came to typify Icelandic culture.

The first settlers brought sheep and horses and cows for work and food. Other than these imports, marine birds were a primary source of food; fish, of various sorts; and marine mammals, mostly whales and seals.[14] Whaling required resources most people didn't have, and a beached whale offered a protein jackpot that fed a lot of people for a long time. If you are hungry and you find a beached whale that has gone a bit off, you eat it anyway. Now you can understand the tolerance for hákarl in Iceland's past.

Looking into the distance from the lighthouse, I thought of the great appetites of nations, the appetites of human beings, and the relationship of our appetites to those melting glaciers. What Freud knew, and what we all know at our core, is that we are driven by unconscious desires, desires of the body and mind. We do not control them so much as manage them, and mostly we fail at that. I wasn't sure about Icelandic culture, but American culture includes a Janus-like tension between Puritanism and hedonism. Just ask any undergraduate at a conservative university: wild abandon on Saturday night followed by ardent repentance on Sunday morning. Freud taught us that when you repress powerful desires, they eventually burst forth with greater fury and destructive power. I thought of the fierce Norse warriors known as berserkers, tasters of blood, who fought in a trancelike state so powerful that fire and iron could not harm them.

Deep in the night, Scott and I were plucked from sleep by three drunk men shouting and shaking tents in the campground. I peered through the tent door. Two of them wore lopapeysas, Icelandic wool sweaters with decorative bands circling the yoke; all three carried beers. They raged and yelled in their drunkenness, howled and laughed like hyenas killing babies.

"They're berserkers," Scott said. "I should get out my can of mace and go after them."

"Yeah," I said. "You should, but that stuff might really mess them up."

"You can kill a man with bear spray," Scott said, "but this mace is for dogs."

I watched through the zippered door of the tent as the berserkers faded into the illuminated night.

Day arrived, and on our way into town to catch the ferry we stopped again at Meistarapylsur. Scott ordered the 14-2, and I went for the Henrik, a "deep-fried hot dog with garlic sauce, Doritos chips, sauces, melted cheese, and spice."

It looked like it was going to be a pretty good day.

Eating the Pylsur of Heaven, Part Two
FROM STYKKISHÓLMUR TO BRJÁNSLÆKUR

Breiðafjörður stretched into the blue distance as a cold wind came up that afternoon over the ferry stern deck. It was hard leaving behind such excellent sausages, but if our luck was right we'd find more down the road. I pulled on my beanie and rain jacket against the cold. Taking up a bench while Scott hit the head, I fished out a portion of Icelandic licorice from the top of my pack. I had seen it for sale everywhere and naturally had to give it a try.

"Good choice," said a middle-aged woman sitting across from me. She wore a heavy wool sweater and tall rubber boots. Her face was deeply creased, probably by the wind and cold. "Icelandic licorice is the best in the world."

"Is everything here the best in the world?" I said. "Best lamb? Best hot dogs? Cleanest water on earth?"

"It is," she said. "Our lamb and hot dogs are unrivaled. You can drink the water right out of any stream. Our hot water comes directly from the ground. It's never ending, so you can shower indefinitely. And we've won three Miss World titles from the pool of our little population. Our women are gorgeous." Then she paused and considered. "But don't eat too much of that licorice all at once. It'll give you terrible farts."

"I'll be careful," I said.

She winked at me.

Scott and I planned to spend the night on Flatey, a complex of some forty islands, the largest of which (Flatey proper) is about two kilometers long and four hundred meters wide, with nary a hill to be seen. The people of the region have long been known for their love of books. A literary monastery (now gone) was established on Flatey in the twelfth century, and in 1864 a library (still there), which once housed the *Flateyjarbók* (Flatey Book), or *Codex Flateyensis*, one of the greatest of Iceland's medieval saga manuscripts. Written between 1387 and 1394, the *Flateyjarbók* includes the *Grœnlendinga Saga*, which tells the story of the Vikings' discovery of Vinland, or North America.[15] The church near the library is more contemporary, consecrated in 1926. For the better part of a thousand years, Flatey supported a bustling fishing and farming culture, part of a rich complex of island life and industry in Breiðafjörður. Historically, the quality of life was better here than in other parts of Iceland due to the productive waters of the fjord and the productive soils of the surrounding land and islands. Today Flatey is the fjord's only island with year-round inhabitants. Some five or six people live here in winter, seven when a visit by a friend is delayed indefinitely by foul weather. The small homes clustered around the hotel that make up the village are mostly summer residences, their privacy compromised by the daily disembarkation of travelers from the ferry. I imagine that residents don't mind too much, however, as it's partly tourist money that makes it possible to live here. Without tourism, this would likely be yet another island with a once-glorious past, abandoned to time, decay, and marine birds.

When the ferry came in on Flatey, Scott and I loaded our packs and walked the dirt road to a farmhouse, where we paid for a tent site in a fenced enclosure. We set up behind a guest cabin, out of the wind, leaving the open grassy field to fill with other travelers from the boat: a cyclist, a group of young French mountaineers headed for the Hornstrandir, and some others who seemed to drift in on the wind. I could feel evening coming on, a subtle shift in the day's light and temperature as the sun came closer to the horizon, a softening like the slow transition of a color print to sepia. But it wasn't going to get dark. It was summer near the Arctic Circle. I set up our stove to cook supper. On the menu, a packaged pasta alfredo dish cooked with a can of tuna, a bit of onion and kale mixed in, enlivened with cayenne pepper. On the side, multigrain crisp bread, then a dessert of chocolate digestive biscuits and hot tea. And to cheer us as we cooked, Brennivín.

Ah, Brennivín, that clear, unsweetened heaven—a distillation of potatoes flavored with cumin, caraway, and angelica—which is the national drink of Iceland that Icelanders (we were told) don't too often drink. In fact, they drink far more Coca-Cola and coffee. The per capita consumption of both is among the world's highest. Brennivín means "burning wine," but it is also known as Black Death, not to be confused with the plague, or the dark beer by the same name that Scott and I drank in Stykkishólmur. It's an essential chaser when eating hákarl, and it is drunk ceremonially with a feast and the recitation of poetry during Þorrablót, the midwinter festival of sacrifice held in honor of Þorr, my favorite Avenger. And naturally, it is drunk when cooking tuna pasta camped on a low island in the middle of a fjord, and it is best to drink it still wrapped in its brown paper bag, as we did.

After our hearty supper, we thought we'd make a walking tour of the island, up the grassy way to the dirt road, northeast along a row of village houses and past the old barn with the sod roof flanked by a windmill tower. Such vibrant color in an Icelandic village, homes of corrugated sheet-metal siding, painted in bright blues and reds and greens, teal too, the color of the sky. It was nearly ten p.m., but the lights were still glowing in the windows of Hótel Flatey and the fabulous restaurant within.

I had a look at the menu posted in the window to lament the delights we passed over that night for our simple backpacking fare. A set menu of blue mussels from the fjord, fillet of lamb with blueberry salt, a "little surprise from the kitchen," potato cakes, and hot rhubarb delight with whipped cream. Or marinated lumpfish roe on blini (a Russian pancake folded like a crepe) with sour cream and onion, pan-fried cod from the fjord with lobster sauce and potatoes, that surprise again from the kitchen, and a chocolate cake with whipped cream that the chef called "With the Sun in Your Heart."

So much of human life centers on food, and so much the better when that food is thoughtfully and lovingly prepared. The words for such dishes are a poetry melting first on the tongue and then in the porches of the ear, followed by all the other senses we delight in. And one of the primary means for a traveler to better know a place is through its food. "For me there is too little of life to spend most of it forcing myself into detachment from it," writes M. F. K. Fisher, the great American writer, cook, and lover of life. "When shall we live if not now?"

We walked on, beyond the village where the brown road became a green path. I could see all the way to the end of it, to a low rocky promontory spinning with aerial birds, where the path turned to the southwest on the opposite side of the island. If we kept on, we'd make a loop and arrive back at our camp, but a sign ordered us to go no farther. The end of the island was closed this time of year, a nature preserve for nesting birds, among them snow bunting, common eider, mallard duck, common snipe (there really is such a thing with feathers), red-necked phalarope, and the invulnerable arctic tern. We paused a moment, happy to comply, taking in the glorious light, the breeze, the promising wild of Flatey Island, then started back along our way. We walked easily along, sharing a tune that came to mind, minding our own business, when, quite suddenly, we were set upon by arctic terns that flew screaming in clouds, swooping and chirping and rushing at our heads. I looked up in time to see one hovering before me, squaring me up, measuring the distance and shape of the wind, and then the dark menace of its gaping cloaca, perfectly timed to drop a substantial shit that floated in a perfect arc straight for me.

"Aaahhh," I called out, dropping my left shoulder as I wheeled away. "I think it got me."

"Let me see," Scott said. "No. It didn't get you."

"Yeah, I think it did. I heard the strike. Look again."

"Nope. I don't see anything."

"Are you sure?"

We were set upon by arctic terns that flew screaming in clouds.

"I'm sure."

"Here comes another one," I said.

"Damn," Scott said. "Berserkers. Let's get the hell out of here."

We kicked it up double-time trying to outdistance them, these white-and-black birds on the wing. But it turns out there is no outdistancing an arctic tern. In 2007–2008 Danish researcher and photographer Carsten Egevang led an international team to track arctic terns on their annual migration with a tiny geolocator tag. What he discovered had been understood but, until then, mostly undocumented. The arctic tern makes the longest annual migration of any animal on earth, from its summer nesting grounds in the polar north (which includes Iceland) to the polar south (primarily the Weddell Sea near Antarctica), a journey of more than seventy thousand kilometers. In a lifetime, this bird may travel the equivalent of three round trips to the moon. Among his discoveries, Egevang found that on their journey south, the birds don't fly straight to Antarctica but hang out in the middle of the North Atlantic for nearly a month to feed. The area is characterized by what Egevang calls "cold, highly productive northern water and warmer, less productive southern water." The collusion of these two currents creates a region of "high eddy variability," a "hot spot" where fish and other sea life congregate, a great oceanic grocery. During all this time, all this distance, arctic terns rarely, if ever, land or sleep but remain in flight. Egevang told me that swifts can stay aloft for up to two hundred days without rest, and he believes arctic terns "can perform something similar." What's more, he notes, the arctic tern—nesting during the polar summer and wintering during the austral summer—experiences more sunlight than any other creature on earth, prompting him to call it "truly a bird of the sun."[16]

As Scott and I crossed the boundary of their nesting site, the attacking arctic terns seemed to melt into the air, but I still imagined them there, their long easy wings pulling up on the wind, hovering and bobbing in the sky over our heads. I could not help but wonder what these seabirds were seeking by making such immense journeys to the ends of the earth, always in sunlight, always on the wing. What force drove them to fly so far for so long? When I posed this question to Egevang, his answer was food. Arctic terns are perfectly evolved to exploit these hot spots in the North and South Atlantic and the fecund polar seas. And yet, even as I know they are after fish, it is hard not to think of these birds as feeding on light from the great proximal star that is our sun, the engine that feeds us all.

Our walk took us out to Flatey's church, where we gazed upon a painted mural of island life: fishermen at their work, ewes with their lambs, and what appeared to be Jesus wearing an Icelandic sweater. We walked on, past the library, and returned to our camp. Scott and I brewed mugs of hot tea and huddled next to our tent out of the cold wind, watching the light linger in the northern night. Near eleven p.m. a group of young women appeared on the grassy field, carrying meat and vegetables and beers, and fired up a charcoal grill. One worked at the hotel, and her friend had come for a visit with her baby. Apparently it had been a long time since they met, as they talked joyously over the cooking and eating of food.

In the morning we took the ferry to Brjánslækur to catch the bus to Ísafjörður. Coming up the road from the ferry terminal, the stench of dead fish blossomed in the air. We walked along a row of industrial buildings, from where the smell seemed to be emanating. This really was the fish basket of Iceland.

We gazed upon a painted mural: fishermen, ewes, and Jesus wearing an Icelandic sweater.

"I wonder what's going on in there?" I said.

"Slaughtering fish," Scott said.

We watched the French mountaineers hit the road, thumbing for a ride, and then stepped into the coffee house where we would buy our bus tickets. The Sterna bus, a small and relatively new company (the arctic tern belongs to the genus *sterna*), awaited us.

"That bus there? No," the old woman said, shaking her head. "No bus to Ísafjörður today until five p.m. Maybe seven p.m."

"Isn't that the bus parked just outside?" Scott said.

"It goes to another place first," the woman said. "It comes back in the evening and then goes to Ísafjörður."

In retrospect, we should have hitchhiked as the French were doing. Or taken the bus to wherever it went, then back here to the ferry terminal. At least we would have seen some new country. But we decided to wait.

We waited. We read. We waited. We played a few dozen hands of a card game Scott called Dirty Oyster (I mostly lost). We waited some more.

"We might as well get a pylsur," I said, noticing a man putting in his order at the counter. "You want one?"

"Yeah, I guess so," Scott said.

The old woman pulled two hot dogs from the steamer and laid them into their fluffy white buns. We loaded them up with ketchup, mustard, and sweet pickle relish. They did not look like the glorious dogs in Stykkishólmur but a bit more like the poor, weak wieners you buy at high school sporting events in America. Still, maybe the combination of beef, pork, and lamb made these dogs superior even without the pomp of deep-frying and baked beans and Doritos chips. We tucked in.

"Not really that good," Scott said.

"No," I said. "Not really."

"I guess all pylsur are not created equal."

"Nor are all pylsur equally created," I added.

"What does that mean?" Scott asked. "What's the difference between created equal and equally created?"

"I see your point. How about another game?"

"Yeah," Scott said. "Let's play. It's going to be a long afternoon."

Let's Take the Bus, Part One
The Neatnik
FROM BRJÁNSLÆKUR TO ÍSAFJÖRÐUR

*I traveled about largely by bus and am convinced that it is
one of the best ways of seeing the country.*
— W. H. Auden and Louis MacNeice, *Letters from Iceland*

Everybody knows train travel is superior to all other modes, except for travel by foot ("It is rich in details," a Hungarian friend told me, who happened to be walking around the world), and perhaps travel by camel (the romance of the Silk Road and all that), and maybe by canoe (because, to me, canoes are a kind of poetry). Except for those three, trains are superior. But I also love my diesel pickup with its seven-foot Alaskan camper. So except for those four, trains are best, and the list of great wanderer-writers who love trains is long indeed. "Trains are for meditation," writes the late Scottish poet Alastair Reid. "I like trains," writes Australian author Anna Funder. "I like their rhythm, and I like the freedom of being suspended between two places, all anxieties of purpose taken care of: for this moment I know where I am going." The 1982 Nobel laureate in literature, Gabriel García Márquez, called the train, through one of his characters, "a kitchen dragging a village behind it." And novelist and travel writer Paul Theroux, a man well known for making long journeys by train, writes, "Ever since childhood . . . I have seldom heard a train go by and not wished I was on it." Because "I can't make my days longer," he muses, ". . . I strive to make my days better."

But we were traveling in Iceland, which doesn't have trains. I don't know why, when the Ring Road circumnavigates the country and seems an obvious route for a train. Imagine how many happy tourists (some of them wanderer-writers) might more happily part with their money while riding the train around the island. Communities on the Ring Road Railway could decide if they wanted to build track outward from the ring to fabulous peninsular destinations.[17] A circular rail line with rays emanating into the peninsulas, not unlike a flower with its petals. Of course, one complication is that a volcano pops its top in Iceland more often than now and again, and the result can be a torrent of glacial melt—especially in the south from Vatnajökull—that rushes out to sea and destroys miles of highway and many bridges. Perhaps Iceland decided against a rail line long ago because rebuilding all that track would be one more expensive thing to do.

Anyway, there are no trains, so Scott and I traveled by bus to various jumping-off points for our backcountry walks. Icelandic buses are fairly nice: no real crowds, slow but acceptable Wi-Fi, and big comfy seats. Not cheap, mind you, but a good option if you decide against renting a car. We thought we might meet some interesting people too, but it wasn't the other passengers who were particularly interesting. It was the men who drove the buses.

Long ago I grew weary of waiting for the world to end, so it made some sense to travel to the end of the world, and in Iceland that would be the Westfjords, the wild and glacially incised region in the far northwest pressing west-northwest into the Denmark Strait. It is a place entirely to itself. Legend has it that a couple of trolls tried to dig a canal across the neck of it to separate it from the mainland, thereby making it into an island. As these things go, the trolls were so devoted to their work that they did not notice the sun coming up and turned instantly to stone.

Grimsey Island, on the east side of the Westfjords, is the site of their tragic end.

The Westfjords are the last best place in Iceland, and anyone considering a walking tour should bring it to the front of their list. Scott and I planned to make a four-day walk into the remote Hornstrandir, and for that to happen we had to take the bus to Ísafjörður. The ferry terminal at Brjánslækur is a nowhere place, merely good anchorage for boats with a small station and coffee house to rest at while waiting for the bus, which, as you know, Scott and I did for seven hours. So when the bus finally arrived, we gratefully got on.

Our driver was a slight man, if that, withery and willowy, who seemed to carry the excessive weight of a nihilist on his shoulders, all the truer by the look of his eyes, which were overshelved by bushy black eyebrows. He spoke no English, rare in Iceland, and it was odd that a man transporting travelers for a living did not have this skill.

Also on board were two Belgians, women of quiet confidence and good humor. They would go as far as Þingeyri (about half the distance we would travel), where the Viking Festival was soon to kick off in celebration of the Viking Gísli Súrsson, the subject of *Gísli Súrsson's Saga*. Briefly, the story is that "Gísli is exiled when he takes revenge for the killing of his wife's brother, by killing his sister's husband," writes Jane Smiley in *The Sagas of Icelanders*. It is "a classic outlaw saga, and dwells with exceptional insight on the inner torment of its central character." Also of note: Þingeyri has some of the best remote hiking in the Westfjords in the overhanging mountains. I almost suggested to Scott that we disembark with the Belgians to take in the festival, walk a few trails, and travel on to Ísafjörður after that. Air travel has you separated from the world, since you just watch movies and drink red wine, but traveling by bus, you come to realize how much of the world there is, and how much of the world you are passing by. You can't follow every shiny thing you fall in love with, though, or you'd get no work done at all. Your entire life would be like a long and glorious party. And who wants that?

So we were off and away on the bus to Ísafjörður, and just a few kilometers down the road we turned north at Flókalundur, home to the Hótel Flókalundur, named for Viking Hrafna-Flóki Vilgerðarson, who sailed to Iceland in 868 (a couple years before Ingólfur Arnarson) and set up a camp at Vatnsfjörður in the Westfjords. Flóki and his party's settlement failed because they did not store enough winter hay for their livestock. Before returning to Norway, Flóki climbed a high peak and looked down into a fjord, the present-day site of Ísafjörður. It was so filled with drift ice that Flóki named the entire island Ísland, or Iceland. It's always good to know the origin of a name.

From here, the bus climbed up and up as we left the pavement for dirt track, skirting the edge of the Vatnsfjörður nature reserve and away into the highlands, a vast expanse of open country covered by a hard crust of broken rock. I sat bolt upright in my seat gazing onto that mysterious land. It was as travel writer Pico Iyer has written, a landscape so primitive and wild, so rife with a mythic shimmering, that I really did expect to catch sight of the monster Grendel shambling among the stones and the hero Beowulf riding out upon his horse.

It was then that I noticed the bus was climbing at ever-increasing speed. Not only were we angled steeply up, but we were going really fast. I checked my GPS: 1,100 meters elevation, 80 km/hr; 1,200 meters elevation, 90 km/hr; 1,300 meters elevation, 100 km/hr; and on up we went, climbing into the sky. We topped out at 1,700 meters elevation and came fast across a long flat where we passed two poor sops on bicycles, their light clothing slapping in the cold wind. The bus kicked up quite a bit of dust, a long contrail running out behind as we descended on the other side, dropping fast into Arnarfjörður, the tight, steep dirt track curling and bending. Our driver seemed not at all disturbed or aware of the road's tight curves, as he pressed harder on the pedal and moved us on at alarming speed. I could see his face in the rearview mirror, the creases drawn down his cheeks into the flat plateau of his mouth, yet I could not see his eyes beneath the bushy country of his brow. He appeared a kind of mad scientist, or was that Groucho Marx at the wheel, whose blood had been recently en-cocktailed by the plasma of Mario Andretti?

Across the aisle, Scott looked at peace, casting a languid gaze onto the shimmering land.

"We're going pretty fast," I said.

"Yeah, we are," one of the Belgians said. "This guy must really know the road."

"I bet he drives it every day," the other Belgian said.

That was some comfort at least as we descended to the sea. Our driver slowed then and turned into a parking lot, where before us was the cascading loveliness of Fjallfoss, a one-hundred-meter-high falls that some consider among the jewels of the Westfjords.

"Take a photo?" our driver said, his only English.

We all hopped out and did as commanded, then hopped back on, and we were off again, running out the remaining klicks dragging our contrail of dust, the driver pressing down and around each curve until in Þing-eyri at last we reached smooth pavement. The town sits at the edge of the water on the south side of Dýrafjörður, protected by a spit of land pushing into it. I found it an appealing place, away from the chaos of the world but with good access to the sea and a dependable road coming in and going out. It looked like the kind of place a guy could put by a stock of supplies and happily await the end of the world. The bridge across the fjord was behind us now, so we'd have to backtrack a bit to continue on to Ísafjörður.

The Belgians stepped off at the station, leaving only Scott and me for the journey onward. But onward is not where we went. Our driver made a few turns onto various streets in town, then backed into a carwash stall and stepped out.

"What's he doing?" Scott said. "Is he gonna wash the bus?"

"No," I said. "That would be silly. Why would he wash the bus with passengers still onboard?"

"He is," Scott said. "He's going to wash the bus. Look at him."

Our driver seemed not at all disturbed by the road's tight curves.

We could see the determination in his face, his bushy eyebrows winking as he went.

He dropped a few coins into the machine and selected the high-pressure prewash. He picked up the instrument and wetted down the roof and hood, the panels and wheels, the back window and bumper.

"What the fuck," Scott said. "I don't want to sit here while he washes his bus. I'm paying for this. I want to get to Ísafjörður."

"Maybe he's just going to spray it off," I said. "We picked up a lot of dust on that gravel road."

"I hope so," Scott said. "Otherwise, we could be here an extra half hour. Or longer. It's getting late, man, and we got some miles to travel yet. I want to get in there and get a beer and then go to sleep."

"Let's hope he just sprays it off," I said.

After spraying it off, our driver changed the setting to the foaming brush, selected the instrument, and started in on a slow and deliberate cleansing, scrubbing away the dust and grime. We could see the determination in his face by the force and care of his scrubbing, his bushy eyebrows winking in pleasure as he went. Scott and I came to call this bus driver the Neatnik.

"Look at him go," Scott said. "What. The. Fuck."

"Okay, wait, wait," I said. "So we're in Iceland on a long bus route to Ísafjörður, and the driver has just stopped halfway to wash his bus. I'm just registering this."

"Is it just me, or is this highly irregular?" Scott asked.

"I think this is highly irregular."

"Yeah, take a photo or something. I mean, does he expect us to just sit here while he washes the bus?"

We just sat there while he washed the bus.

"Maybe he has a date or something," Scott said. "Why else would he need to wash the bus? Why can't he do it after he drops us off? Maybe he's gonna get in there to Ísafjörður and head over to his woman's place and he wants a clean bus."

"Or his mistress," I said. "Maybe that's it."

"Yeah," Scott said. "Yeah. Maybe his mistress. So he's gonna drop us off, and then he's gonna pull into her place, and he wants his bus lookin' real good."

"He's really washing it up nice."

We watched him work the foaming brush, scrubbing here and there, a hard little back-and-forth motion over the trouble spots, so intent it seemed his whole life depended on it.

"Let's be practical," I said. "Maybe this is the only car wash around, and the company requires the bus to be cleaned before it's stowed away for the night. So he has to do it here."

"Yeah, no, this guy ain't doing this for the bus company," Scott said. "He's gettin' laid tonight for sure. Or he thinks he is, anyway, and his bus gotta be clean."

"He's been out on the road, man. He's like a mariner come in from the long crossing."

"Hey, dude," Scott said to the driver. "Wait, wait. Over there. You missed a spot."

"I think he heard you."

"Yeah, look. He went back for it. That's it. Get that spot there too," Scott said, shaking his head. "I can't believe it. I just can't believe what's going on here."

"It's unreal," I said. "But he'll go into the rinse phase soon, and we'll be on our way. I can taste that beer now. It's waiting for us up there in Ísafjörður."

"No, dude," Scott said. "After that, he's gonna have to go with the wax. Really give her a good shine. This is gonna take a while."

And he did. He added more coins, ran the rinse and then hit the wax, covering the clean surface of the bus with a shimmering shine. I had to admit, at least what we could see of it, the bus looked pretty snazzy.

"He's done a great job," I said.

"He sure has," Scott said.

The Neatnik climbed into his seat and pulled the door shut, and at last we drove onto the open road. I felt that we had been through a thing, and we were finally on our way. I relaxed a bit seeing the town pass by on one side of the bus and the fjord on the other, but we went only a short distance before turning into a neighborhood of small, brightly colored houses.

"This doesn't look right to me," Scott said.

"Nope. I'm looking at the GPS, and we're not headed toward Ísafjörður. We gotta go back the other way."

The Neatnik drove up to a green house and backed into a parking spot across the street next to a van. He got out.

"Now what?" Scott said.

"This is probably his mistress's place," I said.

"I'm not sure if I hate this guy or I'm starting to admire him," Scott said.

The Neatnik went up to the house and knocked on the door. No answer. He knocked again. He paced about in a circle. Still no answer. He returned and opened the door of the van parked next to the bus. He opened the jockey box and looked inside. He looked under the floor mats. He ran his hand up along the dash through a clutter of papers.

"What's he doing?" Scott said. "Is he looking for the keys?"

"If I'm gonna be reasonable, it seems to me that he doesn't want to drive this big bus all the way to Ísafjörður with only two people on it. So he's going to swap out for the van, and whoever lives here works for the same company and was supposed to leave the keys for him."

"No," Scott said. "There's nothing reasonable about any of this."

The Neatnik stepped out of the van and made a call on his cellphone. No answer. He returned to the house and knocked again. He paced about in a circle. He came back and tried the phone again. Nothing. He rifled through the van, looking everywhere he could think of.

"What the fuck," Scott said. "I want to get to Ísafjörður."

Outside the bus, the Neatnik paced about in a circle. He looked at his phone. He paced. Checked his phone again. Then something must have shifted in his thinking because he got back into his seat and started the bus, and off we went.

"We going the right way now?" Scott asked.

"Yep," I said, checking the GPS. "Looks like we're on our way to Ísafjörður."

It was nearing eight p.m. and the sun had fallen a little lower in the sky, that continual twilight of an Icelandic summer. We hummed along at an easy pace, and I felt the happiness of moving on toward our destination. Then the Neatnik's phone rang.

"Damn," Scott said. "What if we have to go back?"

"Damn it," I said.

The Neatnik spoke rapidly in Icelandic. He seemed to be having an argument, and it escalated until he cut the conversation off and put his phone away. We did not turn back.

"Yep," Scott said, nodding. "His mistress can't see him tonight, and he washed his bus real nice and everything. And for what? For what? A rough day for this dude."

"Yeah," I said. "A rough day for all of us."

Into the Hornstrandir, Part One
AROUND ÍSAFJÖRÐUR

Who has gone farthest? for I would go farther
— Walt Whitman, "Excelsior"

n Hesteyri, a collection of summer cabins near the mouth of Hesteyrarfjörður, the leftovers of a failed fishing and farming effort from a century ago, Scott and I met a couple coming out of the Hornstrandir as we were headed into it. Presumably a married couple, British, in their early sixties, visibly shaken, their faces pulled down as if they had just slipped past death. They wore rain gear despite the clear sky and the bright sun pitching off the water.

"You've certainly got a good day to start," the man said to me.

"We do," I acknowledged. "A great day."

He stared at me, saying nothing, and in saying nothing begged for me to ask him something. It was obvious that he had a story to tell, a story about something he and his wife had passed through. He looked annoyed by the world that was failing to notice. Whatever drama unfolded out there, whatever terrors they faced, whatever joys, the world had gone spinning on and, with the exception of some people close to him back home perhaps, nobody cared.

"We didn't have a good start," he finally offered. "The weather came in. Terrible rain. Terrible wind. A fog in the passes. We couldn't see anything."

"We couldn't see anything," the woman repeated, coming up behind him.

"That's right," he said, shaking his head. "We couldn't see anything. I thought we'd never find our way out. It was so empty. So desolate. We were lost for some while and we couldn't see anything."

To consider that kind of isolation, that kind of fear, he let a silence build between us again, standing there at the waterline of the fjord, the boat we came in on bobbing on the gentle waves, dockside. The moment passed as the breezy clouds formed and broke apart, and the waters came into their blueness, and the birds sang in the palace of summer, buzzing with summer insects.

"Come on," the woman said to him, making a move for the boat headed back to Ísafjörður. "Let's get the hell out of here."

There wasn't much for Scott and me to do but adjust our packs and set out, walking up the long track along the fjord into whatever weather, whatever darkness, whatever light. It was near four p.m., a late start, but at this latitude it wasn't going to get dark. We had all night in daylight to get to our first camp.

Scott and I would walk the Royal Horn, a well-established route through the Hornstrandir. The boat had dropped us at Hesteyri inside one of the five fjords tucked inside an even greater fjord called Jökulfirðir. Day one would take us over a high mountain pass and down the other side into the Bay of Hælavík, facing north onto the Greenland Sea (16 km). On day two we'd walk the beach to the foot of another high pass, descend the other side, and climb again, up and over, descending into the Bay of Hornvík at Höfn (15 km), where there's a ranger station and one of the world's great seabird cliffs, Hornbjarg. On the third day we'd climb over our final high pass and descend into another great fjord, Veiðileysufjörður (15 km), where the boat would pick us up on the fourth day.

Going for a walk this way, four days stretching before you, your gear stowed in your pack—your food and stove and tent and bag, with a map and GPS to guide you—you feel the long reach of the cities pushing at you, the discourteous thrum of traffic and industry, the foul air and the noise of the dispossessed. You feel it pushing you, driving you to the perimeters of the world where you have only a thin edge to walk, a precarious strip of quiet and solitude coupled with the kindnesses of some few other walkers.

The Industrial Revolution has made the walking tour a nightmare, as all roads became high-speed corridors of goods and services and death. It is more and more difficult to find a good place to walk, alone or with an old friend, and you often have to travel far to find it. This was not so when the poet Wordsworth, in a fit of youthful delinquency, left the comfort of his studies to roam the Alps on foot. Or when the writer Stevenson led a donkey through the Cévennes. Or when the greatest American walkers set out: Thoreau; Whitman, the poet of the public road; and Lewis and Clark, who also journeyed on horseback and by boat. In those days, nothing on land moved faster than a horse, so all roads were foot roads too. But these days, to travel on foot it's best to seek the places at the edges of other places where the wild country is, where now all walkers must go.

Walking up Hesteyrarfjörður, Scott and I angled toward a bright snowfield where the British ranger at the landing had told us to go, picking our way through steepening fields of boulders and using our trekking poles for support. We did not find a path so much as a lightly worn discoloration in the rock, an occasional boot print in a chance pot of sandy soil, a dirty sight line across a snowfield, a string of great rock cairns drawing out the way. Over the wider, flatter passages along the treeless rim-top of the fjord, the defeated snowpack formed streams that fell away into the sea far below. Sometimes we crossed by skipping from stone to stone, other times by stopping to change our shoes for sandals and wading the frigid, fast-moving runnels. This, Icelanders claim, is the cleanest water on earth, so we drank freely without filter or compunction.

We rose to the final push of our first mountain pass, Kjaransvikurskard, just below Geldingafell (598 m). At the base of it, Scott and I stopped. The way up was covered in snow and much steeper than we were prepared for, as we wore simple low-top walking shoes without hard

"We go up," Scott said, and up he went.

edges. Our feet were already bruised by the hard stones of the path. The snow arced above our heads, breaking over the broad back of the mountain saddle, a ramp into the sky.

"Which way do we go?" I asked, as if it needed saying.

"We go up," Scott said, and up he went, kicking a stairway into the snow with his light shoes and pressing up with his legs under his heavy pack. I watched him rise a few steps ahead before I followed. Though others had gone before us this season, the sun strike on the exposed snow face erased all traces. It was as if we were the first men on earth to ascend here.

The way was slow going, and with the weight on our backs a slip or a moment's hesitation would send us tumbling down the mountainside. We would likely survive such a fall, if we rolled well and somehow avoided a cracked skull, but it would certainly ruin the day. We beat out a rhythm, kicking in a foothold and stepping up, kicking in a foothold and stepping up again. To look up was to risk losing my balance, so I mostly kept my head down. Listening to the sound of Scott above me in the interstices of my own kicking and stepping, I moved up ever slowly, hoping my shoes would keep their place in the snow until Scott drew away and then vanished over the top. I went on, feeling a strange emptiness bind up in my heart, the slope curving away from me, the ground flattening beneath my feet, but it was here, as my lot began to improve, that I felt a twinge in my right leg, a weakness at the next step. Was my knee going to buckle? Was my leg going to give out? Was this a message from the muscles and bones of my body or from the temperature of my convictions?

I did, in that moment, imagine falling, the twinge in my leg breaking loose at the joint as the pack's weight pulled me back, my head landing me upside down as my feet came over into the sky, and then, in my mind, the view from some other place of my broken body at the bottom where the snow turned to rock, exposing the bones of the mountain.

But I did not fall. I pressed and stepped, pressed and stepped, pushing that pack up the slope until I found myself standing on relatively flat ground next to Scott. We paused to look out onto the fjord far below, a blue line that widened into Jökulfirðir and around Snæfjallaströnd to Ísafjörður, where we had started earlier that day. Our walk into the Hornstrandir had just begun.

What causes loneliness, especially loneliness while traveling in foreign lands, that skip or catch in the breath, and then the sink of the heart from a place of exaltation to the darkness of fear and loss? What is it? As a younger man discovering the wild landscapes of North America—the Frank Church wilderness in Idaho, the canyons of southeast Utah, the endless boreal forests and lakes of northern Saskatchewan—nature was a balm to me. It was in wild places that I felt closer to the divine, as close as I could feel anyway. I am not a Christian, and though I believe in prophets, I do not believe in a loving god, nor do I believe in a religion that persecutes and executes and burns in the name of a loving god. Even still, out in those vast wildernesses I felt the presence of something greater than myself, and that something, I felt, knew me. I wanted to believe in that something when I was in other places too, but I never found any evidence to support it. None. No sign or symbol or voice out of the whirlwind. Just silence, enduring, empty, black silence. Prayer, I learned, is an impish wish, a childish fantasy as selfish as two opposing football teams on bended knee, each with the same ardent belief that God is on their side. The older I get, the more certain I am that there is no "spirit in the woods," as Wordsworth asserts. There is no hand of god to guide me. Everything does not happen for a reason, but rather, given enough time, everything will happen for no reason at all. The longer I live, the more I am convinced of nature's utter indifference to human wishing and human suffering. And at some point in my travels, I came to feel that this indifference is beautiful, that beauty is an aesthetic of bleakness, of the black emptiness of cosmic space. In imagining tumbling to my death in the Hornstrandir, I did not look to god in nature to comfort or save me; rather, my only refuge was the beauty of these lands, and traveling in the company of my old friend.

We walked it out from cairn to cairn all the way to the sea.

We descended. Down the other side of the mountain pass, walking at a good pace, the northern sun waning in its arc but not falling, a colder air coming in over us. We sweated and beamed and delighted in the power of our legs, the ease soon to come to us, for we could now see all the way to where we would camp, the shining waters of Hælavík facing the Greenland Sea. I began to think of the rum and vodka we'd brought, spirits that might lift us in this cold, desolate, beautiful place in which we now darkly walked. The fjord was a series of great benches carved by a long-forgotten glacier, and as we came off one bench and then another, more great benches were revealed. After an hour of walking, Álfsfell (584 m) rising above us on the east and Fannalagarfjall (618 m) on the west, it appeared we were no closer to the bottom. It felt like we were walking the wrong way on an escalator.

"Is it just me or are we not getting any closer to the bottom?" Scott said. "Isn't it just right there?"

"It looks right there to me," I said. "I can see it."

"Got to be," Scott said. "But it isn't getting any closer. And I'm wrecked."

"Yeah," I said. "I'm ready to stop too."

Strange how light worked in that country under evening summer sun, that this series of benches made our destination look refreshingly near, but it was painfully far. Perhaps the angle of our sight line allowed these long benches to appear stacked, one on top of the next, and foreshortened this way gave us a pleasurable false hope.

We pressed on, our quads and knees and feet bearing the weight and jounce of our walking, and the hard stony ground come up under us, battering the bruising in our feet. The path was clearer now, and in some places it became a trail, and we walked it out from cairn to cairn all the way to the sea. The beach sound roared in against us, and that fresh sea air, and at the first wide, grassy place where other walkers had camped, we threw down our packs and shucked off our shoes. First order of business: a slug of spirits to toast our long, good day.

"Damn," Scott said, raising his cup to mine. "I'm beat."

"Nice to have a clear night, though," I said. "Happy it's not raining."

"True," Scott said. "I'm beat, but the good thing is, I'm dropping weight. We got worked today."

"Right. You got to be. I'm probably dropping weight too."

"Did I tell you I'm down to 230 now?"

In high school and in his early twenties, Scott had been a talented athlete: football, basketball, track, and rugby. But a few years ago he'd hit an all-time low by hitting an all-time high of 265 pounds. His gut spilled over his buckle, and his face became fleshy and soft. It looked like he was headed for more weight too, and the many problems that come with it—diabetes, heart disease, immobility, chronic joint pain, not to mention low testosterone and sexual dysfunction leading to a general distaste for life. But something awakened in him, and he put himself on an exercise regimen and improved his diet. Instead of a flash weight-loss gimmick, he lost weight by simply burning more calories than he took in. Over the past year, a major motivation for him was making this trip.

"Damn, 230," I said. "Would you say this trip saved your life?"

"Yeah, it saved my life," Scott said. "It gave me something to work toward. I needed that. My long-term target weight is 195, and a couple of years ago that felt impossible. But I'm going to hit it."

"That's fantastic."

"Yeah," he said. "I'm feeling fucking fantastic, and fucking fantastically too." He paused. "But lucky for you, Caswell, sleeping next to you so many nights in this tent, my libido is at an all-time low."

The sun moved sidelong behind a headland, and the temperature sank. It was ten p.m. We put on our rain gear against the cold, set the tent, and sat in the lee of it to cook a simple meal of tuna pasta with onion and broccoli, crisp bread, and chocolate digestive biscuits. While we ate, two figures emerged from a tent we spotted on the hill. They stood into the wind held in each other's arms, seemingly impervious to the bracing cold. A postcard you might send home.

Into the Hornstrandir, Part Two

AROUND ÍSAFJÖRÐUR

Morning came to the Hornstrandir, and I crawled from the tent to stand in the light of the hesitant sun. The shore was white with driftwood, a great logjam of giant trees built up on the beach—mostly larch, fir, spruce, and poplar—speckled with colorful fishing floats that had come in from the sea. Where did all this wood come from, since Iceland is mostly devoid of trees? Out of the forests of Siberia, carried down those great rivers that flow into the Arctic Ocean: the Lena, Ob, and Yenisei. Traveling four hundred to one thousand kilometers a year, such logs remain at sea for at least five years. The saltwater cures the wood, toughening it, and the longer it remains adrift the tougher it becomes. The early settlers of Iceland used driftwood for building shelters and homes, boats, furniture, food bowls, barrels, boxes, and for making charcoal. Driftwood belonged to the landowner and was often branded like livestock. The Icelandic sagas include stories of disputes and negotiations over driftwood caches. Of particular note, during the Middle Ages, witch burning was not so much based on an abundance of witches but on an abundance of wood, especially driftwood. When the Christians had a good supply of wood, witches who needed burning seemed to show up everywhere.

I returned to the tent to join Scott for coffee and a simple breakfast of muesli cooked in water, sweetened with honey. The sky looked fairly steady, though overcast and gray. We broke camp, loaded our packs, and set out.

Auden proclaimed the Westfjords the most beautiful part of Iceland, and the Hornstrandir must be its greatest virtue. It was the last region to be settled in Iceland, but the few hardy farmers and fishermen who tried to make a go of it were gone by the 1950s. Winter travel was too difficult, with access only by boat (as it is today), and the short growing season coupled with a slow recovery after grazing made keeping livestock a zero-sum game. In the fjords, seasonal polar ice made fishing dangerous and unsustainable. In 1975 Iceland declared the region a 58,000-hectare nature reserve and national monument, thereby protecting some of the world's greatest seabird cliffs and marine mammal habitat and offering a last refuge to the arctic fox. Elsewhere in Iceland, foxes are hunted and killed as vermin. Not so long ago an occasional polar bear drifted from Greenland to these shores on pack ice, but even as the guns of the sheep ranchers are gone from the Hornstrandir, climate change makes it unlikely that the region will ever see another.

The Hornstrandir is part of a great basalt plateau dramatically inscribed by fjords and bays and short valleys eroded by glaciers. The plateau rises four hundred meters from the sea at Aðalvík in the west, and up to seven hundred meters in the east at Hornvík (where we were going), though to look at it you see not the plateau that has long since eroded away but a vast and wild landscape of rugged and misty mountains. The bedrock here is 14 million years old. Cirques, amphitheater-like valley heads, are characteristic of the region. Climatic features include prevailing northeast winds, a mean annual temperature of about 3.5 degrees Celsius, and annual precipitation of roughly 1,250 to 1,350 millimeters. Polar winds push onto the northern coast, which is a mere three hundred kilometers from Greenland.

During the most recent glacial maximum (eighteen to twenty thousand years ago), the Hornstrandir was largely covered by an ice cap that extended some six to ten kilometers beyond the coastline.

The shore was white with driftwood,
a great logjam of giant trees.

The plateau's highest points, however, were buried not under glaciers but under perennial snowfields, or firns, a conditional stage between snow and glacier. Such high points in the Hornstrandir were dotted with nunataks, exposed ridges or rock features surrounded by these firns, and ice-free slopes between glaciers and the plateau edge. After some ten thousand years of advancing and retreating, deglaciation of the Hornstrandir was complete by about 9,500 years ago, leaving behind a dramatically changed landscape. The remnant glacier, Drangajökull, is the country's only glacier not currently in retreat. With its volcanic and glacial activity, Iceland, and subsequently the West-fjords, is a prime location for rheology, the study of the flow of matter. To the human eye, such mountainous landscapes are fixed, but across immense spans of time they move. Mountains do walk, as the ancient Buddhist masters have always known. "If you doubt mountains' walking," the thirteenth-century Zen master Dōgen writes, "you do not know your own walking."

Walking the shoreline that morning, we made our way along the easy breakers as they came, pushing us up the beach. As the water drew back out to sea, so did we, walking a smaller wave pattern along the waves, along the wrack line, mindlessly, really, angling down onto the harder black sand where the surf would soon be and then back into the drier, loose sand where the waves pushed us. There was no path on this section of the Hornstrandir, and barely a path anywhere in the whole of it, certainly not through the basaltic boulder fields, which kept no foot-prints and resisted wear, and not through the clean, white fields of snow, whose paths were momentary.

A good path is not made to walk but made by walking, as poet Antonio Machado has written. And a path made by walking is the keeper of all walkers' dreams. You have to be careful, walking in a landscape like this, that you do not trod on another's story. You walk alongside it, paying homage as you pass, as you make a story of your own, whose outcome cannot be known while walking.

You do not ask or strive for meaning. You just walk; walking itself is the meaning you strive for. If someone asks you what you learned out there, it is best to answer that you learned nothing at all. You just walked, and that is enough. You walked, and by walking you became part of the place you walked so that a place that was not a place to you before you walked it becomes inseparable from your identity. It becomes part of who you are, part of your body and your mind, and as such, your mind becomes another wild place to walk in. You walk along the edges of the world just as you walk along the edges of your thoughts, and thereby into the strangest country. The real journey is inward, the thought of which you must keep very quiet, lest those who are threatened by such ideas invest considerable energy to unhinge you.

I have never made a first ascent of a great peak, or a first descent of an impossible river, or sought to travel the knife edge between life and death. Such adventuring, while it makes a fabulous story, has become routine. Everest, for example, that peak of human desire, has become a commercial industry. You pay and then step into a vast and bulky line to do what so many others are doing. The real journey, I think, is not in feats of derring-do but in paying attention to a place, to the outward details, the sights and sounds and weathers, and to the inward details, to the deep and quiet places of the mind and of the heart. Once home, the great adventure is in writing the story of your journey.

The quiet beach that morning led toward a distant headland dropping sharply into the sea, and beyond it a massive cirque, white with snow, running up to the sky. I looked down at my feet and noticed fox prints in the sand, two sets, one going out and one coming back. The set going out appeared to be running, as the prints were deeper, more distantly spaced, the animal going on along the sea at a charge. The set coming back, a quiet saunter, a morning wanderer, out for a look around. Perhaps they had passed here at different times, or was this the same fox twice, with different intentions? I stopped, as Scott came up behind me, and we both considered the track of the fox on that silent beach, our own footprints too, leading away from the camp we'd left behind.

Every road leads in two directions—where you've been and where you're going. Since where you've been is not possible to get to, we had no choice but to walk on.

I checked the map as we approached a complex of small houses and buildings, apparently a private inholding, likely a failed farm from long ago that the family refashioned as a summer retreat. When Collingwood and Stefánsson traveled here, people were still trying to make a living off these remote farms. As they sailed by on their schooner, the pair regarded this coast as "inhospitable" and characterized its people as "the least known and most forlorn of Icelanders. . . . They have to wait for weeks or months in winter before they can get to church to be baptized or married, or to bury their dead."

The sun warmed through the misty clouds, and a sweeping path worn through the grass led us through the center of the old farm. At the edge of an outbuilding three young arctic foxes rolled and played in the northern sun breaking through the clouds. Little brown things, fuzzy and round with pointed ears and black eyes. All three ran for the cover of the front porch to let us pass.

We walked on, and as we walked, we began to realize the great cirque in the distance was our path, the first of two mountain passes for the day. I could now see the trail switchbacking across what looked like a challenging climb. The scooped bowl of the mountain covered in snow where only mountain goats, and maybe the foolish, might go. We rose off the beach, up and up along the trail. The way was clear and easy if you paid attention, but narrow and exposed with nothing to stop your fall. We climbed steadily, not talking. I was grateful for my trekking poles to steady me, which I had purchased in Ísafjörður. And happier still for my merino wool underlayer, wind jacket, and trekking shorts, which I wore over a pair of black wool knee-length tights. On colder days like this one, I pulled my long black ski socks up so they met my tights at the knee.

We came over the top of the pass called Skálarkambur and down the other side. The way became lost to us through the boulder fields; we found it again, then lost it once more. The cairn in the distance pointed the general direction, but we could not stay on the path. It was here now under our feet and then out over there as we walked beside it, so faint as it wandered through the landscape. Like the waves on the beach, always shifting, or like a photon of light, which according to Heisenberg, is not in one place at any one time but shows a probability to be here or over there. Judging by the path's faintness, the impact we might have on this landscape was so minimal as to be nearly nothing at all. We were like ghosts walking a ghost trail through the black fields of stony rocks. "O you and I who never have existed," writes the Icelandic poet Steinn Steinarr, "One instant, like a shadow on a wall, / Appears the image we were destined for."

A snowfield appeared before us, and we crossed it, following the dirty boot prints of other walkers. It was nearly impossible to keep from kicking snow into my low-top walking shoes. I paused again and again to finger it out, my socks growing ever wetter. I soon learned that if I walked more slowly and deliberately, making a wide step with bowed legs, I could keep my feet drier. We walked mostly in silence, Scott and I, as it was too difficult to talk and negotiate the snow and boulders, and the weather, which came in tight against us. We pulled our hoods up to keep our heads dry.

Walking these treacherous paths, I thought about the early Iceland-ers who traveled here, how they negotiated these passes in search of good ground to plant or a grassy swale to graze their sheep. Did they find the divine in these mountains and seas? Or did they feel as I do, that beauty arises from the divine's absence? Perhaps such settlers did not cross this particular pass at all and it was a crossing only for walkers like us.

Unlike so many modern nations, Iceland was uninhabited in the ninth century when Norse people arrived, except for some Irish monks, who (god bless 'em) thought Europe too crowded for their taste. Thus the nation has no dark history of supplanting a people already here, unless you consider the millions of birds and fish and marine mammals taken to feed a growing population.

The Norse who sailed out from mainland Europe in longboats car-rying their sheep, goats, cattle, and gods (especially Þórr) must have thirsted deeply for something new, for someplace new where they might establish a civilization of their own. Theirs were largely economic pressures, as most of the good farmland on the mainland was already occupied, and some few nobles fled the policies of the tyrannical king Harald Fairhair (AD 850-932). And yet to choose that option, to set sail on a dark and mysterious sea in relatively small boats, must have required a measure of courage, along with desperation or even madness.

The passage from Norway to eastern Iceland took seven to fifteen days, if the weather was good. A stop in the Faroe Islands would extend the duration, as would a journey to western Iceland and present-day Reykjavík, where nearly two-thirds of Icelandic people now live. Often the weather was not good and the crossing treacherous. How many boats and people have gone down to a watery grave in the North Atlantic?[18]

In AD 1000, when Iceland named Christianity its official religion, the Norse gods went quietly underground. Such a choice, I think, offers a key insight into the way Icelanders came to regard this land, which I heard Icelandic novelist Auður Ava Ólafsdóttir characterize as "this mysterious black island" at a reading in Reykjavík. Perhaps Iceland was just too dark and cold for too much of the year, too bleak and empty to go on for long without the comforting illusion of a loving god. To ward off that awful loneliness of winter, nature had to be animated, and conveniently, Christianity was franchising in the neighborhood. This is the choice most of humanity has made, adopting the comfort of religious doctrines, which promise some sort of everlasting life to stave off the bleakness of an indifferent universe.

To find a sentient creature that might have lived otherwise, we must go back further in time, beyond the settlement of Iceland and onto mainland Europe, as far back as forty thousand years ago, when Neandertals lived alongside modern humans. According to evolutionary anthropologist Steven Churchill, Neandertals were robust human beings with great barrel chests, stout bones, and an impressive musculature. They were able to withstand cold and well suited to carry heavy loads. "Neandertals were more muscular than are most living humans today," he writes, in *Thin on the Ground: Neandertal Biology, Archaeology, and Ecology.* With this greater musculature came greater strength. Today a reasonably fit 200-pound man can bench press about 90 percent of his body weight, or about 180 pounds. Neandertals would have far exceeded that. "Make no mistake: the Neandertals were strong," Churchill writes. And they were incomparable walkers, walkers of the most exquisite type, whose livelihood and daily life as hunters and foragers shaped their physicality. According to a study by anthropologist David Raichlen and his colleagues, Neandertals had taller heels, making their foot structure and musculature highly suitable to walking.[19] Their heavy brow ridge, large and powerful lower jaw with retracted chin, and relatively large nose and nostrils gave them the appearance of that iconic apelike brute we associate with stone-age humans.

But Neandertals were not apelike brutes. They were humans like you and me. A number of researchers, Churchill, and also Svante Pääbo, head of the department of evolutionary genetics at the Max Planck Institute for Evolutionary Anthropology, have discovered that Neandertals likely possessed the power of language, or at least communication; they developed complex tool-making processes and may have adorned their bodies with hematite, or red ochre pigment. They buried their dead, suggesting some belief in an afterlife. It was once thought that modern humans drove Neandertals to extinction by outcompeting them and possibly killing them. This is true, but Pääbo's work has shown that the two species were so similar that they interbred, and since modern humans outnumbered Neandertals ten to one, we became the dominant and only remaining human species. The evidence is in us, as most Europeans carry Neandertal genes today.

There is a key difference between modern humans and Neandertals, however. Unlike us, Neandertals did not make much art. It was long thought that they were not capable of art, but we now know that they were. "Neandertals were capable of symbolic expression," Churchill told me. "They were occasionally making items of personal adornment. Even though they weren't making much art, it wasn't because they weren't capable of doing so." Nor were they plagued by restlessness, or whatever it is that pushed modern humans onto the seas to colonize distant continents and islands, else Neandertals might have peopled Iceland long ago. "It's only fully modern humans who start this thing of venturing out on the ocean where you don't see land," Pääbo told Elizabeth Kolbert for her book *The Sixth Extinction*. "Part of that is technology, of course. . . . But there is also . . . some madness there. . . . How many people must have sailed out and vanished on the Pacific before you found Easter Island? I mean, it's ridiculous," he said. "And why do you do that? Is it for the glory? For immortality? For curiosity? And now we go to Mars. We never stop."

Neandertals did not take such extravagant risks. They did not venture onto the hostile seas, and they did not make art. And why not? Perhaps one reason is that they were solely nomadic, a hunting-gathering culture devoid of aspirations for permanent settlement. The choice for such cultures, as Jacob Bronowski affirms in *The Ascent of Man*, is "starve or move." So they moved not into the unknown, not into the vast seas of the North Atlantic, but along tested pathways during specific times of year when they knew food plants and animals were certain to be found. And in such moving, civilization is impossible. What you can carry is limited, and you would not make things you could not carry, nor would you develop the ability to make them. Nomads, Bronowski asserts, do not even make memorials, for "nothing is memorable. Nomads have no memorials, even to the dead . . . the only mounds that they build are to mark the way." So what "happens to the old when they cannot cross the last river?" Bronowski asks. "Nothing. They stay behind to die. . . . The man accepts the nomad custom; he has come to the end of his journey, and there is no place at the end." In this way, for nomads, "the adventure leads nowhere. The summer pastures themselves will only be a stopping place . . . there is no promised land."[20]

The story of the Promised Land, the seminal work of which is the Hebrew Bible, is the story of a nomadic people transitioning to an agrarian economy, a transition that modern humans would complete but

Neandertals would not. Abel, the keeper of sheep, a nomad, is murdered by his brother Cain, a tiller of the ground, a farmer. It is Cain who takes control of the lands Abel formerly roamed and there founds civilization on a farming-based economy. The Hebrew Bible is about the birth of civilization through the development of agriculture, and then the buying and selling of land. It is the myth that parallels the story of the meeting of modern humans and Neandertals.

Without art, then, without a capacity or a need for metaphor, without the madness that drove modern humans to leave their homes and sail the open seas in search of something they may not find, it seems to me that Neandertals may have lived more simply, more at ease in the sheer presence of light and warmth, food and sex and companionship, the immediate comforts and pleasures of the body. I don't mean they experienced these pleasures all the time, but they lived for them instead of living for the promise of an afterlife. Without the need for metaphor, was it not easier for Neandertals than it is for us to live in an indifferent universe? If you consult *Gilgamesh*, the world's oldest written story, you find the selfish and narcissistic worship of individual power, which leads to such a fear of death that the protagonist, Gilgamesh, king of one of the world's first cities, embarks on a journey of folly: the search for immortality. He fails in his quest, of course. Unlike modern humans who are, even in the twenty-first century, seeking what Gilgamesh would never find, perhaps Neandertals lived simply and easily in the body's needs and pleasures, however briefly. In an indifferent universe, perhaps it is easier to be mostly indifferent yourself.

Into the Hornstrandir, Part Three
AROUND ÍSAFJÖRÐUR

Scott and I reached the bottom of Rekavík into Hornvík and pressed on around Einbúi to Höfn camp. At one point we used fixed ropes to help us over a steep hump of rock along the beach and walked a foot trail overlooking a sharp precipice falling away into the sea. Seabirds—puffins, black guillemots, and arctic terns—spun along the sea cliff below us.

Höfn was a busy place. The Icelandic ranger was in his cabin, and a few groups of twelve to sixteen people were camped on the flat. We counted more than twenty tents. We found services here too—a WC with flush toilets, a couple of pit toilets, and a sink tapping water from a spring.

We pitched our tent against inevitable rain, cooked again in front of the tent door, and drank off the edge of our sore muscles and aching joints. An arctic fox made a pass to test us for handouts. The sign near the spring reported that feeding foxes is all right, but please no sweets.

"I'm tired," Scott said.

"Me too," I said. "But maybe we should walk around the horn to see the birds?"

"Birds?" Scott said. "All I've seen for days is birds."

"Yeah, but this is supposed to be one of the greatest seabird cliffs in all the world."

"We should stay here and drink the rest of this vodka," Scott said.

"Maybe so," Scott said, "as dramatic as that is. But I'm all broken."

"Same here, but we should probably do it. I doubt we'll ever make it back here again."

"Probably not," Scott said. "In fact, I'm surprised I made it here this time. I bet you were sitting around in your house wondering who would be dumb enough to think this was a good idea. Cold. Wind. Rain. Birds shitting on you from the sky. You were looking for someone dumb enough to say: yeah, okay, Caswell. I'll walk all over Iceland with you. You were asking that question, and the answer you came up with was me."

"That's right," I said. "And here you are."

"Yeah, here I am, and now I'm all broken. I can hardly stand up, and my little toe is mangled and purple. How am I going to walk out on this?" he said, inspecting the puffy little sausage.

"Yeah, that doesn't look good, but that's why we should make the walk out there to the horn," I said. "It'll loosen us up."

"No, we shouldn't. We should stay here and drink the rest of this vodka," Scott said. "And besides, I'm not as dumb as I used to be. I'm coming to understand, after thirty years of friendship, that you're just a bit crazy."

"Am I?"

"Yeah, just a little bit."

"Okay," I said, hoping to sound less crazy. "Let's stay put. I've seen plenty of birds too. And why didn't we grab that deck of cards from the ferry terminal? We could have another game of Dirty Oyster."

"Yeah, why didn't you think of that, Caswell?"

"I don't know," I said. "And it's likely that nobody will ever use those cards again. They'll just sit there in the terminal forever."

"Yeah, 'cause nobody else is dumb enough to get stuck in that place for seven hours."

"Here," I said. "Let's pour out a bit more." I emptied the vodka bottle into Scott's cup. "That's the end of that one."

"Good thing we're not staying on here another few days. We're out of alcohol."

"No," I said. "We have a bit more rum."

We sat up a while longer until the sky came down to squat on the flat and the rain popped against the tent fly.

"Well," Scott said, after we'd crawled into the safety of the tent, "I'm going to sleep."

"It's a bit early, isn't it? I mean, it's like 8:30 p.m."

"Yeah, it is. But you know what? At 9:30 it will still be light. And at 10:30 and at 11:30, it will still be light. So, what does it matter what time it is when I go to sleep?"

"Good point," I said.

"Yeah, it is a good point," Scott said. "And besides that, you know what?"

"What?" I said.

"I'm going to sleep, 'cause there's nothing to fucking do."

He bore the countenance of a man who'd lived his life outdoors.

It rained most of the night. I woke again and again to the rain, a light mist, a heavy thrumming, a break, then a reopening of the sky. By morning the rain lifted and we crawled from the tent to a world soaked in cloud and mist. The mountains we would soon cross, to our south, were occluded by cloud, and white runnels poured off the face into the great wetland below. I was sore and stiff from all the walking, from carrying my pack, and we had another hard day ahead of us.

"It's all wet outside," Scott said, because someone had to say it for us both.

I made coffee, and we cooked up the muesli, added our honey, and ate and talked about the day. As we packed our wet tent, the ranger walked up and gave us his name: Jón Björnsson. In these parts, we later came to understand, he was a bit of a legend. He might have been sixty-five, perhaps older, a beanie with a tassel on his head, a light jacket, and cotton pants tucked into his knee-high rubber boots. His face was bright and open because this rain was nothing to him, nor these dark clouds menacing a storm. He bore the countenance of a man who'd lived his life outdoors, an easy, wiry look, and hard as nails.

"Good morning, gentlemen," he said. "You are heading out today?"

"We are," I said.

"That is very good. It is best to get an early start. It will be heavy rain in the afternoon. It is best to be on the other side."

"We'll be on our way shortly," I said.

"Very good," he said. "You are taking the boat then, in the morning?"

"Yes," I said.

"I will be joining you on the boat."

"Oh, great," I said.

"Not great," he said. "I must go to a funeral in Reykjavík. It's a sad story, you know. But Icelandic funerals, there is a lot of alcohol. So it won't be too bad."

"What time will you start up the trail today?" I said.

"I will go in the morning."

"In the morning?"

"Yes. The trail is little problem for me."

"And you probably know the way."

"Yes, I know the way. I could walk all of it backward." He smiled. "Well, you best be getting on. This here is the most direct trail. Easiest for you. I will see you in the morning."

We finished loading our packs and set out, walking the easiest route for us and ascending a high bench above the flat, crossed and cut by flowing waters. The mists that hovered above us set down on the back of the mountain, and the higher we climbed, the closer we came to the clouds. Soon we were shambling along inside the clouds and through the mists where we crossed several snowfields, so bright in the dark air we put on our sunglasses. In places we did not know if we were on the route or not, and then a cairn came into view at the limit of our sight, so we walked to it. Arriving at the cairn, we followed a dirty footpath through the snow, trusting that in time we'd see another cairn, which we did, just as we began to question where to go.

Walking these paths, it was easy to become disoriented and get lost in the boulder fields. The GPS would show us the way, but if we were delayed and the batteries ran down with no sun to charge it, what then? Crawl into some deep hole in the rock for shelter and wait for a clearer day? These cairns, like sentinels, one after the other, appeared when we needed them most. Still, what separated me from the complete loss of my bearings was not the wish or belief in these stone guides but the permeable membrane of friendship, my companion who, if needed, would put out a hand in the dark.

We walked on and on, until our path turned sharply up, the final hump to the saddle of the pass. We ascended, pushing up the pathway to the top, 515 vertical meters from our camp. At the summit pass the wind pushed and beat us, coming cold out of the mist and dark. At my feet I discovered fox droppings set down in an X on a stone in our path, and next to it a collection of tiny white flowers bending in the summit wind.

Making a journey like this is difficult, I have learned, because each time you set out on a journey, you sever your ties to home. You do not know—not really—when you'll be back, or even if you'll get back at all because you don't know what might befall you on the road. You leave your warm house for the bright world, moving along from place to place, and with each place are new possibilities. Above all else, new possibilities are what hominids desire most: a new day, a new chance, a new place. "Wayfaring," writers Merlin Coverly in *The Art of Wandering*, "is the fundamental mode by which living beings inhabit the earth," and "the act of walking becomes a means of reading a landscape."

Scott and I walked and read out the signs that would lead us through, the dirty tracks over the snowfields, the thick, squatty sentinels of the cairns in the mists, the swirl and spin of the clouds, until we came out on the other side where we descended at an angle across a steep snowfield, down, down, until we dropped below the clouds at last and a blue sky greeted us in a bright day. From here, like the day before, we could see our way down the long, slow slope across the boulders to the waters at the head of Veiðileysufjörður. My heart warmed and felt at ease, as it appeared that we were almost home. "He who enters it is lost," writes Ibn Battuta, that twelfth-century prince of travelers, "and he who leaves it is born."

Yet the way seemed to resist our going, for when we reached the bare rock below the sharp, snowy descent, we found no more cairns to lead us. The problem was not that we could not find our way, as the waters of the fjord were in sight, but that we would not find our way easily. We struck out across the pathless lands, keeping watch for piles of stones. We skirted around great boulders, over streams and their companion patches of mud and swampy grass, and back to the boulders before us. In time, what looked like a pile of rocks became a cairn, and back on track, we followed the faint path down. Behind us, storm and cloud spilled over the pass and filled the void below, pushing us down the fjord to the water. Out of the distance, a younger walker overtook us, a Frenchman with a big camera, and he beat us in to the safety of our camp.

We found a depression in the ground to pitch our tent and tied out the wind anchors, setting them firmly in the ground. We cooked and ate as the sky grew darker, and just as we finished up the dishes, the rain came down the fjord. The wind forced the rain against the fly, bending the tent poles in.

The rain came down the fjord on the wind.

Seated there in the tent in the storm, I made my notes on the day. The journey is not over until you have told its story, I wrote. I sketched a picture of our tent in the wind, regretting the angle we had pitched it. A little more that way, the narrow end more into the

The journey is not over until you have told its story, I wrote.

wind, would ride out the storm a bit better. No matter. Scott woke from a troubled sleep as I wrote, the tent bending and luffing in the wind. "Here," he said, "I'll just press my big ass up against the wall of the tent so we don't blow away."

Rising to the light of day, I saw that it was not raining anymore. I stepped out of the tent to find two new tents in the camp, late arrivals in the stormy night. A seal lifted its head from the waters of the fjord. I watched it bob away in the waves. After coffee and hot cereal, Scott and I waited inside our tent for the boat—"it is best to leave up the tents," Jón the ranger had told us; "the boat can be delayed for many hours"—and then, quite suddenly, we heard the voice of the man himself. Jón walked into camp with a small pack on his back, still wearing those rubber boots.

"Did he walk all that way in those rubber boots?" I said to Scott.

"Damn," Scott said. "I bet he did."

"Good morning," Jón said. "I see you arrived all right."

"We did," I said. "What time did you start walking?"

"I departed at about eight a.m.," he said.

It was now 10:30. What had taken us most of a day to walk he had accomplished in two and a half hours.

"Now that's walking," Scott said.

I wondered what the Hornstrandir felt like to Jón, who negotiated its steeps and boulders and snowfields with such ease, its stream crossings and marshes and bogs, the beach sands, the grassy swales running up the fjord bottoms, the winds and rains and snows of summer. He must feel perfectly at home in the land, and if so, did that feeling come from outside him, from the place itself, or from inside him, a feeling he created? If the land was empty, if nature is indeed indifferent, perhaps it is still possible to love a place, to love a landscape, when love is projected onto it. Perhaps when we cast the net of ourselves into the void, instead of drawing it back in we might leave it out, so that next time there is a there to go to.

The boat appeared in the fjord, the white line of the wake trailing behind it. Scott and I broke down the tent and packed it away. We still had a good string of days to explore the north and east of Iceland, and as the boat pulled in I was ready to move on.

Let's Take the Bus, Part Two
The Sleeping Giant
FROM ÍSAFJÖRÐUR ALMOST TO AKUREYRI

After our walk into the Hornstrandir, Scott and I recovered for a day in Ísafjörður. News came in from Scott's wife back home in Oregon that their young daughter was in general defiance of parental authority. She was in the middle of those years when the body is a riotous cacophony. Under such conditions, parental authority is what you're going to defy. But there was little Scott could do from Iceland. He bore that troubling news like a champ as we moved on from Ísafjörður to nearby Súðavík (we walked the first ten kilometers; a friendly motorist gave us a ride for the second ten) to have a look at the Arctic Fox Center. We found no foxes at the Arctic Fox Center but rather people who love them and a café where I enjoyed a coffee and a piece of rhubarb cake before we caught the bus to Akureyri, the center of human life in the north of the country.

Akureyri is due east from Súðavík, but we would have to ride the bus south to Borgarnes and transfer to another bus that would take us north and east on the Ring Road. Our route was shaped like a check mark, and a long one at that. We would not get in to Akureyri until near midnight, at which point we would still have to find the city campground, set up camp, cook dinner, and then have a nip of something to take off the edge before we could rest. So, do you see what I mean about trains? If we had been riding the rails all that way, it would have been a genuine pleasure, walking from one car to another, looking out windows onto the wild lands, sitting in the dining car and dining, and having a nip of something to take off the edge.

Despite what Ester Rut Unnsteinsdóttir, head of research at the Arctic Fox Center, had told us in the café—"People don't come to Iceland for sun; they come for other reasons"—we had sun that day, and gloriously so. Unnsteinsdóttir also told us that a dead orca had washed up on the beach not far from where we had camped in the Hornstrandir, a jackpot food source for foxes. But foxes are no match for the tough skin of an orca, so they wait for the beast to rot before they eat it.

When the bus pulled in to take us to Akureyri, we hopped on in the spirit of adventure, our packs well provisioned with stove and stove fuel,

They wait for the beast
to rot before they eat it.

cookable food, water, spirits, and a few tasty sweet granola bars Scott had christened "snacky food."

The route out of the Westfjords followed the shoreline of a series of fjords off Ísafjarðardjúp, in and out, out and in, like tracing the fingers on your hand. A young French couple, our only company on the bus, she a quiet beauty with perfect dark skin and a nice backpack, and he a rugged, modestly handsome fellow, wiry like a climber, who smoked each time we made a stop. We rode it out, the group of us, as the sun glinted off the palace of the waters, those long slips of blue inlet each an outlet to the sea.

Our driver stopped to pick up a woman standing by the edge of the road. She sat in the jump seat, that little seat in front of the great eye of the windshield reserved for tour guides, but she spoke only to the driver, in Icelandic, a long and uninterrupted string of words entirely unintelligible to me. She and the driver seemed to know each other. Perhaps it was for the best, her talking on the way she did, with all that warm sun striking our driver in the chest, as it might otherwise be difficult for him to stay awake, something I now wrestled with, nodding off from time to time.

We reached Borgarnes around eight p.m. Our driver showed us to the next bus, the one headed to Akureyri, more than three hundred kilometers away. We had already come nearly four hundred kilometers, and we were pretty tired of the bus. Not to mention that it seemed our drivers had fashioned a deception so we would overpay. We bought three tickets each: from Súðavík to Hólmavík (home of the Museum of Icelandic Sorcery and Witchcraft), 5,500 krona ($41); from Hólmavík to Borgarnes, 5,500 krona ($41); and from Borgarnes to Akureyri, 10,400 krona ($77), for a total of 21,400 krona ($159). The bus from Hólmavík to Borgarnes stopped in Bifrost, a good thirty kilometers from Borgarnes, where we might have jumped off, had a brief rest, and caught the bus to Akureyri, saving us a good hour of bus time and sixty kilometers of bus fare. But this is all in retrospect, and the complaint of someone who has been on a bus too long. So in Borgarnes (again) we boarded the bus for our final leg of the journey.

The French couple boarded with us but stepped off at Hvammstangi on the Vatnsnes Peninsula, probably for seal watching at nearby Hindis-vík, an impressive sea stack that according to nearly everyone is actually a petrified troll. The troll, the story goes, was so preoccupied in its mission to destroy a local monastery that it didn't notice the rising sun, which turned it into stone.[21] There is a lot of this going on in Iceland. Everywhere you look, your eyes fall upon a rock that was once a troll, which begs the question: how do so many of them get caught this way? You'd think trolls would have learned by now that sunshine is bad for them and so developed better tools to avoid it.

I think it has something to do with the way light works in the northern latitudes. Situated between 64 and 66 degrees north latitude, Iceland has a seasonal cycle of dark winters and light summers, instead of a daily cycle of night and day. At the height of summer, from mid-May to mid-July, the sun rises at about four a.m. and sets at about eleven p.m., but it does not get dark. To get dark, the sun must drop below 18 degrees of the horizon, and during these months it never drops below 6 degrees. The light at this angle is known as civil twilight, sometimes sweet light or the blue hour, characterized by an absence of shadows and muted visibility. Twilight bends perception, and while you cannot feast your eyes on much of anything, you may feast using all your other senses—sound, smell, touch, and maybe even taste—as you walk the border country between dark and light, between this world and the other.

If I were a troll (which I am not), I would prefer to do my work—like destroying monasteries, breaking into liquor stores, and driving hapless travelers to their doom on buses—during the long summer twilight. It's warmer than winter and the sun is down, but there is still plenty of light. The danger is that you hardly notice when the sun comes up. I can imagine a troll engaged with his work getting caught by the sun, because the quality of light hardly changes from one moment to the next. This is how it must happen for trolls, and it really is a pity. It's a wonder any of them make it beyond those teen angst years without being caught by the sun.

As twilight approached, the French couple stepped off the bus, leaving only Scott and me to make the rest of the trip to Akureyri.

"Hey," Scott said, scrutinizing our new driver as we motored down the highway. "Is this dude driving with his eyes closed?"

"You know," I said, "I was just noticing that."

"Sure as hell looks like he is."

Our driver was a giant of a man, perhaps six-foot four, with a heavy liquid belly spilling over his suspendered black polyester trousers, one suspender clip disengaged at the back, pants drooping on that side. An older gentleman, he had gray, thinning hair, neatly combed so that you could see where the comb teeth had come through it. His long, spacious cheeks and tired eyes made him look sad. When we made scheduled stops at petrol stations (where no one got on or off), he smoked a cigarette outside. From the bus window, I could see that his fly was down.

"Yeah," Scott said, as the bus went on down the road. "This dude is nodding off. Look at him."

"That's not good," I said.

"It's not good at all," Scott said.

We moved closer to the front of the bus for a better look. We watched as our driver's eyelids drooped and shuttered and then opened again in alarm. He drew his big hand down over his face and breathed heavily in a sigh. He had entered that stage when the body convinces the brain that driving with your eyes closed is a good idea. Scott and I came to call this driver the Sleeping Giant.

As the main route around Iceland, the Ring Road is generally well maintained, but it doesn't have much of a shoulder. In many places it's humped into a hillock so that even crossing a long flat, the road might be raised a good ten feet, with big transport trucks coming the other direction at delivery speed, the wind of them shuddering the bus as they pass.

"Hey," Scott said. "Is this dude driving with his eyes closed?"

So head-on with one of those trucks would be a real problem, and if we went off the road, we'd really go off, flying into empty space and dropping like a pheasant plugged by birdshot.

"There he goes again," Scott said. "His eyes are closed, and I'm not ready to die yet."

"No," I said. "Me neither."

"Maybe we should bail at the next stop," Scott said. "Get on a different bus."

"Or just stop for the night, wherever we are. Where are we, anyway?"

We pulled into another petrol station, and the Sleeping Giant went inside.

"Oh, good," Scott said. "He's getting coffee."

He stood in line a moment, paced about, and came away with nothing.

"Nope," I said. "He gave it up."

"Damn it," Scott said a few more minutes down the road. "Look at him. This dude is sleeping. We gotta get off this bus."

"Hey," I said to the driver. "Are we stopping at this next town?"

The Sleeping Giant didn't look back or even acknowledge that I had spoken to him.

"Hey," I said, leaning forward. "Hello? How about this next town? Can we stop there?"

He woke then and turned toward me.

"Any idea about this next town?" I said.

He shrugged and looked onto the road.

"I don't think he speaks any English," Scott said.

"I'm moving into the shotgun seat." I did so, and the Sleeping Giant looked me over. "Do you speak any English?" I said.

He shook his head and shrugged.

"We need to have a pretty loud conversation," I said to Scott. "About anything. Keep this dude awake before he kills us."

"Yeah," Scott said, upping the volume. "BEFORE HE KILLS US. WE GOTTA TALK REAL LOUD, ELSE THIS GUY'S GONNA FALL ASLEEP AGAIN AND KILL US."

"WHY DON'T YOU LOOK IN THE GUIDEBOOK AT THE NEXT TOWN?" I said. "MAYBE WE CAN GET OFF THERE AND FIND A CAMPSITE."

"Yeah," Scott said. "I AM LOOKING RIGHT NOW. DON'T LET THIS DUDE FALL ASLEEP. I MEAN, THIS SHIT IS SERIOUS. THIS DUDE MIGHT KILL US BY DRIVING THE BUS OFF THE ROAD."

Not a week before, I had read *Bill and Dave's Cocktail Hour*, a blog by writers Bill Roorbach and David Gessner. It was "Bad Advice Wednesday," and the subject and title of Gessner's post was "Try Not to Die." It begins like this: "It's hard to type when you're dead." A few paragraphs later, Gessner wisely concludes, "staying alive is a pretty key aspect of the writing life." This made a lot of practical sense to me, and I wasn't ready to let my writing life go just yet by dying.

"Let's bail," I said. "Let's get off this fucking bus."

"Talk loud," Scott said. "Let's keep this guy awake until we can bail."

"What's the next town?" I said.

"Some place called Varmahlíð," Scott said, consulting our guidebook. "Doesn't look like much, but it does have a campsite. And it also has a town pool. We can get a shower in the morning. But even better, it will keep us from getting dead."

"How far is it?" I said.

"It's not far," Scott said. "Like maybe twenty minutes."

"Varmahlíð? Var-mah-leed?" I said to the Sleeping Giant. "Stop in Varm-ah-lid?"

The Sleeping Giant nodded his head.

When the bus pulled into the station, we got off, dropped our packs on a bench, and paused to collect ourselves.

Varmahlíð, I would later discover while studying my maps, is up the glacial valley from Skagafjörður, in the middle of which is Drangey Island, a kind of fortress of rock. Steaming into the fjord, Collingwood and Stefánsson write, "Drangey stood grim and gray upon the water, seeming unapproachable, with bare sides and bare top, the most inhospitable of abodes." Like so many such features, Drangey was formed when two trolls, a male and a female who were lovers, and their cow were caught by the sun and turned to stone.[22] In the sagas, Drangey is also the final retreat of the outlaw Gettir the Strong. After he wounded himself by chopping up a piece of enchanted driftwood, his enemies climbed the ladders up the sheer cliffs and killed him. Clearly, there was a lot going on around Varmahlíð.

"Wow," I said to Scott. "That was a close call. We came pretty close to getting dead."

"It was," Scott said. "I mean, that dude was sleeping at the wheel."

"He sure was," I said, as the bus pulled away into the night.

"Well, I hope he makes it," Scott said. "Wherever he's going. At least now if he kills anyone, it'll only be himself."

"What's our next move?"

"Our next move is that," Scott said, pointing to the Hótel Varmahlíð. "We go to that hotel and get a drink at the bar."

It was near midnight, and inside the bar Scott and I found that the staff had gathered for a party. Food and drinks for everyone.

"We're not open much longer," the bartender told us. "And I am so sorry, but the kitchen is already closed."

"That's quite all right," Scott said. "We just want a beer."

"Just a beer," she said. "Oh, I can do that." She was arranging a huge tray of drinks for the staff. "That's twenty-three," she said. "I just made twenty-three margaritas!"

"Impressive," Scott said. "We were on a bus to Akureyri, but we got off here because our driver was falling asleep. We decided we didn't want to die."

"Oh, dear!" the bartender said. "Well, you two do need a beer, then."

"Do you have Black Death?" Scott asked. "Appropriate for tonight, don't you think?"

"You mean Brennivín?"

"No, the beer," Scott said. "We drank it in Stykkishólmur. Good stuff."

"No," she said. "How about Einstök? I have the white and the pale."

"That will do," Scott said. "I'll take the white."

"A white for me too," I said.

Made in Akureyri, Einstök is the Icelandic beer that claims the distinction of conquering your Viking thirst.

The bartender popped off the caps and handed them over. "Here you are, guys," she said. "Enjoy the rest of your lives."

The Dizzying Heights of Dettifoss
AROUND AKUREYRI

That was a rough day, that bus ride to Akureyri, but the road ahead promised to be smoother, perhaps easier, and certainly safer as we planned to go on foot. Because Scott and I were not yet dead, we thought we'd have a look at Dettifoss by making the two-day walk down the river Jökulsá á Fjöllum (Glacial Mountain River) in Jökulsárgljúfur, part of Vatnajökull National Park. Dettifoss is one of Europe's most powerful waterfalls, made famous in the opening scene of Ridley Scott's 2012 movie *Prometheus*. At 333 feet wide and 144 feet high, a respectable 6,816 cubic feet of water flows over the falls per second. For comparison, Oregon's Multnomah Falls is 635 feet high, and its yearly average high flow is 150 cfs. Scott and I would take a bus east to Ásbygri, walk to Vesturdalur the first day, camp there, and head to Dettifoss the next day, totaling about forty-eight kilometers of foot travel. We stashed our unneeded gear at the Akureyri Backpackers hostel, where we had reserved a room for our return. The route was marked "challenging," and some sources called it one of the country's top ten hikes. After our walk in the Hornstrandir, we were in pretty good shape and thought we'd do just fine.

If you were to see a polar bear in Iceland, you would probably see it in the country around Akureyri, out on the trails maybe or along the shoreline up Eyjafjörður, the fjord the city sits on. Polar bears have long been regarded as possessing magical powers, and they have the ability to appear in one place, vanish, and in an instant appear in another. They come off the drift ice like ghosts and vanish into snowstorms. Collingwood and Stefánsson traveled through this part of Iceland and tell the story of a man named Arngeir who was killed by a polar bear. His son, a man named Odd, tracked the bear down and killed it. Killing the bear made him "shape-strong," and he took on the bear's powers. After killing the bear, he went home, but the next morning he woke at his sister's house, which was a considerable distance from his.

It was raining in Akureyri when we boarded the bus for Ásbygri early that morning. The rain fell steadily and made our view from the bus windows a dreamy mess soaked in a green mirage. I kept drifting off to sleep, the way you do while traveling in the early morning on a bus, even when well rested, and I woke occasionally to stare out at the wild summer openness. Twenty kilometers outside of Húsavík, I saw fields of black lava and a series of upright rock formations, the expanses between them covered in green moss. So strange and eerie were these in the mist and rain that I was certain I had caught sight of a bull with great horns, or maybe it was a troll, silhouetted against the horizon. Farther on we passed sea cliffs swarming in birds, and lava tubes, those dark entrances to a world beyond. Then Icelandic ponies grazing softly in the rain at the ramparts of named and nameless hills. Scott sat across the aisle from me, alternately watching the country and reading Redmond O'Hanlon's riotous travel book, *In Trouble Again*.

It was still raining when we reached Ásbygri, so we lingered inside the station house. We ordered fish soup and bread at the counter and sat hunched over our steaming bowls, hoping the rain would stop. It didn't. It looked to be a miserable day unfolding ahead of us. "Nothing is more suitable to a significant departure than bad weather," writes Paul Theroux in *Ghost Train to the Eastern Star*.

"Well, we're going to get wet," I said.

"Yup," Scott said.

We hoisted our packs, stepped into the rain, and walked across a green flat leading into the mists. The land around us had been so absorbed by the spongy sky that we could not easily get our bearings. It appeared that we were walking in the clouds. Soon my rain shell was wet all over, and the ground, too, was increasingly sodden. The trail became a trench as deep as our knees, overhung with drooping grasses and other greenery. Those grasses directed the rain down our legs and into our socks and shoes. Soon we were as wet from the waist down as from the waist up. We waded through the earth this way for a mile or more expecting the trail to improve. It didn't.

"Top ten hikes in Iceland?" Scott said, to voice our misery. "I'm thinking not."

We slogged onward, getting wetter and wetter with no hope of returning to the shelter of yesterday. I thought of the early Icelandic settlers and how they got on in this landscape without high-tech rain gear. Maybe a wool cloak is the better shield from this unrelenting rain. Or perhaps they just stayed inside in such weather. It wasn't much farther before the cloudy mists began to lift, and we emerged from the shrubberies and that hated wet trench onto a rocky promontory. The land fell away into a great chasm, and far below us ran the river Jökulsá á Fjöllum, spitting and churning and racing toward the sea. The rain had slowed, and the break made it pleasurable to drop our packs for a rest.

This was the landscape where long ago a man called Þorgeir bought a calf from a woman who lived on Hrísey Island in Eyjafjörður. With the help of his kinsmen, he slaughtered and skinned the calf but left the entire skin attached at the tail so that it became an enchanted skeletal aberration, dragging its own skin behind it as it walked, dead but not dead. He put strength in the calf by magic and poured into its bones the essence of air, bird, dog, cat, mouse, man, and two sea beasts, unspecified. With these essences, the calf grew into a great bull that could fly, run, swim, and appear in the form of any of the animals poured into it, including itself. Still not satisfied, Þorgeir draped a baby's caul (amniotic sac) over the bull, making it nearly invulnerable.[23] Þorgeir and his kinsmen called the creature Þorgeir's Bull and used it to carry out dark errands, play tricks, and generally do their bidding. Þorgeir sent his bull against a woman he loved who had rebuked him. He sent it into the fields to mount other men's cows and to make them stampede. He ordered the bull to bring storms down from the mountains to savage the villagers and their fields and livestock. Eventually the bull turned against Þorgeir and his family, who were forced to wear runic charms as protection. At age eighty-six, on his deathbed, Þorgeir woke to find the bull sitting atop his chest in the form of a gray cat waiting for his spirit to depart his body. In this Christianized world of Iceland's past, Þorgeir's Bull was widely regarded as an abomination, an instrument of jealously and hatred, a devil creature befouling the purity of the world God created. The story goes that Þorgeir's Bull is out there still, wandering the pastures in fog and mist and darkness, bellowing, dragging its bloody skin behind it.

After our break, Scott and I trudged on through the rain that slowed and stopped and started again. The rain plagued us all the way to Vesturdalur. Near a picnic table, we pitched our tent and climbed in, both of us sopping in our clothes. The only way, it seemed to me, to recover our sense of humor was to cook. During the next lull in the rain, the mists rising off the green, grassy campground scattered with a few other tents, I sat in the open doorway and set up the stove on the ground.

"Hey," Scott said, reclining inside the tent. "Why don't you pour out some of that rum?"

I did, and it made things a lot better. I cooked up one of our standard meals, pasta with a can of tuna, some broccoli, and the crisp bread. More rum.

After we had eaten, the rain slackened, but it was getting late. Such weird light at eleven p.m. in an Icelandic summer, night but not night, day but not day. When you are two dudes sleeping in a small tent after getting soaked all day in the rain, you find a bit of space to yourself by lying head to toe, my head on the end with Scott's toes, and my toes on the end with Scott's head. We pulled our buffs over our eyes to cut out the summer light and settled in for the night.

We woke to voices, someone bumping the guylines of our tent and the familiar sound of a backpacking stove running on high. It was near midnight.

"Do you like potato mix?" one voice said, in a thick accent. "I like potato mix."

"I don't know," said the other. "I've never had it."

"I must eat a lot," said the first. "I am too skinny."

One of the voices bungled himself up in our guylines again, pulling and snapping the rain fly.

"Oh, I am sorry," said the first, seemingly to the tent. "But this tent is too close. This table is for all to enjoy. It is not for you only."

"Where are you from?" asked the first.

"Australia," said the second.

"I am from the Netherlands," said the first. "And I like potato mix. Would you like to try potato mix? I must eat a lot. I am too skinny. I must gain some bulk for when I go to the swimming pool."

"Who are these clowns?" Scott said. "I'm trying to sleep."

"I have a very high meta-bow-lism," said the first. "So I must eat a lot."

"Is that so?" said the second.

"I'm trying to sleep," Scott said to me. "Can't these clowns cook somewhere else?"

"Apparently not," I said.

"Maybe I should go out and savage them both," Scott said.

"Please do," I said. It was only later that I realized what a blessing Þorgeir's Bull was as a tool against fellows like these.

"I have a very high meta-bow-lism," the first went on, "and I need more bulk for the swimming pool, for the girls you know. But at least I have ah-four-pack. Take a look."

Apparently he lifted his shirt to display himself to the second.

"I see," said the second.

"A four-pack," Scott said. "There is no four-pack. Either you have a six-pack or you don't."

"I am too skinny. For this reason, I like potato mix to gain some bulk," said the first.

This shit went on for some time, these two cooking and eating, mouth boasting, and tripping over our guylines and generally being a nuisance, and Scott swearing he would savage them. Lucky for everyone, maybe, he did not, even as I encouraged him to do it, and it also rained off and on. Maybe they departed when the rain started, I don't know, as somewhere in all that messy chaos I fell asleep. When I woke it was a little brighter outside, and that brightness allowed me to feel a little bit better about the day.

We made the coffee, sipped it slow and sure and happily—me outside the tent making it, Scott sitting inside drinking it. We soon loaded up and walked the trail.

My shoes, soddened by yesterday's rain, were mostly dry and my socks fresh, with yesterday's socks hung on the outside of my pack to dry. We walked and walked, the trail sometimes a trench again through soft hummocks of green shrubbery. We forded the channel of a river after dropping down from the rim. We walked an island in that river to its head, where a small waterfall came in, and then went up the side and over it across a bridge and into the cover of Icelandic birch, low wind-twisted trees deformed by winter storm. Passing beneath that canopy, we crossed a field of riotous yellow and purple flowers. I paused to make note of it in my journal.

Footsore from rock hopping all day in our thin-soled shoes, we turned onto the trail that led us to the paved road and walked into the campground near the parking lot, a moonlike landscape with a few picnic tables and water for backpackers stored in plastic jerry cans.

We selected a spot, set up the tent, and went to work cooking the evening meal. With the stove running and a little something in our cups, I noted the barren landscape and then said, "So, did you hear someone opened a restaurant on the moon?"

"Oh, did they?" Scott said.

"Yeah. Good food but no atmosphere."

A power beyond belief,
a torrent of gray dropping over
the edge of the world.

"Damn it, Caswell," Scott said.

We ate and drank and rested a bit. Thus refreshed, we decided to have a look at the falls.

Dettifoss is a shifting, amorphous flow of glacial waters, a power beyond belief, a torrent of murky gray dropping over the edge of the world with spray rising wildly upward on a wind of its own making, the rim of the falls shaped like a capital J. The river that forms Dettifoss, Jökulsá á Fjöllum, flows from Vatnajökull, the country's largest glacier,[24] and includes a good deal of water rising up from springs. Such glacial rivers fill and swell in summer, especially during sunny weather as glacial melt reaches its annual maximum. In winter they slow and atrophy as freezing temperatures retard glacial melt. As the river's flow changes across the year, so does Dettifoss, surging in summer and shrinking in winter, a patterned rhythm like a lung.

The trail down to it goes right to the edge, with nothing more for a barrier than a thin, frayed rope strung along a few rotting wood posts. Standing there, you feel that Dettifoss wants to carry you over and pull you in. Never in the United States would a traveler be allowed to get so close to his doom, to be so responsible for his own safety. In Iceland, you are afforded the choice to stand back at a safe distance before this terrifying beauty or to step close and fall to your death, if you want to.

Looking onto Dettifoss, I was reminded of something I learned from my reading. Even as the water going over the precipice and forming the falls is never the same water, the falls itself, even as it expands and shrinks season to season, looks about the same. Why is that? In *The Web of Life*, Fritjof Capra describes the workings of a vortex of water or whirlpool. "Water continuously flows through a vortex," Capra writes, "yet its characteristic shape, the well-known spirals and narrowing funnel, remains remarkably stable." Change (the water continuously flowing through the vortex) and stability (the consistent shape or form of the vortex) are known as a dissipative structure. Living systems, too, are dissipative structures. It was Russian chemist and Nobel laureate Ilya Prigogine, Capra reports, who coined the term "dissipative structure" to describe living systems. To be alive means to be in a state of dynamic change. Matter and energy flow through a living system, and while the cells of that system are continually being replaced with new cells, it maintains a stable structure that is recognizable over time. Dettifoss looks like Dettifoss even after a thousand years, just as a person looks like themselves over their lifetime. Returning to the example of the vortex of water, if something disrupts the flow of matter and energy, the structure may reach a state of equilibrium, and equilibrium is death for dissipative structures. However, even as disruption pushes the structure toward catastrophe, it may adjust to find a new stable state before it reaches that point. Capra calls this a bifurcation point, a "point of instability at which new forms of order may emerge spontaneously, resulting in development and evolution." The disruption in a living system that appears to be its undoing (let's call it a wound) may actually result in beneficial change. Looking at Dettifoss, it was possible to understand this, that life is a dynamic flow of matter and energy, moment to moment, and disruptions, our wounds, help make what we are into what we will be.

Back at camp it wasn't raining at all, and Scott and I were feeling pretty good about our day. But just then, as if appearing out of the air, the Netherlander walked up to our camp and dropped his pack at our picnic table.[25] Turns out the Netherlander was traveling with a girl, and she was almost as skinny and annoying as he was.

"Well, for fuck's sake," Scott said.

I couldn't speak at all and glared in the most unfriendly way I knew how. After a time, our two visitors hoisted their packs and went to pitch their tent elsewhere.

We woke to wind and cold and cloudy skies. When the bus arrived, we got on and had an uneventful ride back to Akureyri to check into our room at the hostel. The hostel put us in a room with two bunkbeds to accommodate four people, and when we entered we could see that a roommate had taken one of the upper bunks. I took a lower bunk, and Scott took the lower bunk beneath our roommate. I went to the shower room first, and when I came back, in walked our roommate, a Japanese woman who seemed to be traveling alone. Her hair was wet, and she carried a bundle of wet clothes. Scott went off to the shower. While I was sitting on my bunk doing this and that, our roommate hung her wet towel on the bedpost and hung her sink-washed clothes on the bed rail over Scott's bunk. She hung a T-shirt, a pair of hiking pants, some socks, and then she hung her black panties on the railing. That done, she took up her phone and essentials and left the room.

When Scott came back from the shower, he sat down on his bunk. He looked up and saw the panties drip-drying in front of his face. He looked over at me. Then he looked back at the panties. "Well," he said, "looks like it's time for a beer."

Waiting for the Monster

FROM AKUREYRI TO EGILSSTAÐIR, AND AROUND

At the shore of Lake Lagarfljót in the east of Iceland, Scott and I waited for the monster. From the main road through the town of Egilsstaðir, we had walked a gravel drive to a guesthouse on the lake and then to this secluded spot on a bit of gravelly beach, where even we, who were not paying guests, were unlikely to be disturbed. It looked to be as good a place as any to see a monster, the long, lovely lake leading away in front of us, its glacial waters edged in low mountains to the sky now mostly covered over in dark clouds. It was midday but darker than any clear summer night at this latitude. Scott poured a dram of spirits into our tin cups, because when you are travelers in a foreign land, the break from all routine allows concession. We sat and drank and watched the lake for a ripple or rising form, any disturbance in the water, hopeful for a monstrous shape beneath the waves.

"Do you think the monster will appear?" I said.

"Certainly not," Scott said, "but we should wait for it all the same."

"Right," I said. "We should. We must, because this might be the day."

"As good a day as any," Scott said.

Largarfljótsormurinn, the monster in the lake, is said to be a great serpent, a terrible water worm some three hundred meters long, covered in nasty spikes with great humps on its back. It has lived in these waters a long time; sightings date back to 1345, the age the sagas were written,

109

and as recently as 2012, when a local farmer spotted it from his kitchen window while having a morning coffee. He shot some video footage, and yes, you can find it on YouTube.[26] In 1589 the worm breached the lake's surface and made an arch of itself so high a ship could have sailed under it. In 1987 the monster was seen coiled like a pit viper in the Atlavík inlet near a popular campsite. Other reports claim the monster is even larger, as long as the lake itself, or maybe it *is* the lake, the longest in Iceland at twenty-five kilometers. The lake is as much a lake as it is a wide spot in the river Lagarfljót, which flows from the glacier Vatnajökull down the great and narrow length of the lake, a current snaking through, waving from bank to bank and blown willy-nilly by the wind. Glacial water offers poor visibility, a milky blue or gray distinction of glacial silt, so like all such monsters, Largarfljótsormurinn appears only in the darkest occlusions of its murky home.

Undaunted by our task, and by pouring courage into our cups, Scott and I sat like stoic Vikings at an outpost waiting for the enemy to appear. There was hardly a thing to say, or a thing to say about it, though we went ahead and said stuff anyway.

"You know, Auden traveled here and wrote a book about it," I said, drawing on my recent reading.

"Is that so," Scott said. "Very interesting."

"*Letters from Iceland* is the title, and it's written in an unusual form," I said, feeling professorial. "It's a series of letters home, but many of them are written in verse. Four of those letters are written to Lord Byron, who, by the way, was dead when Auden was writing. Of course, he wasn't the first to try this form. Lord Dufferin wrote a book about Iceland in letters, only his letters were written to his mother. And maybe better is Collingwood and Stefánsson's book about their journey, which is filled with beautiful illustrations."

"Now, see," Scott said, "the other guys aside, how does a book like Auden's get published? An odd form. Written as letters in verse. And to a dead poet, no less. Hardly a travel book at all. And yet it makes its mark."

"Well, he's Auden," I said. "Or he was, for he is now also dead."

"That seems to be it," Scott said, "not the dead part, but the name. Who he was seems more important to the life of his book than the book itself. Politics, maybe. Or fame or fashion. I see a lot of books out there that get a lot of attention but aren't very good. They merely fill a space we've made for some political or social moment."

"But you can't get by on fashion alone," I said, knowing we had no idea what we were talking about. "You have to have a good book."

"Yeah," Scott said, staring at the lake. "It should work that way. You should have a good book, but that doesn't explain all the bad books. Seems to me that writers and their books are marketed these days by who they are, not how well they write. They sell books based on some oddness about them, and if they write angrily about one of the social or political moments everyone is angry about, such a book sells rather well."

"Depressing, but then books have always been positioned in the cultural moment. Take Snorri, for example," I said. "His *Prose Edda* was an attempt to preserve some of the pagan world being lost to Christianity. I doubt it was very popular with Christians."

"Good point. I just hope a writer's success is based on mastery of craft and not personality or scandal or whatever the news cycle is pushing."

"Good point," I said.

"What I'm afraid of is that we're fomenting a culture war. We're so distracted by ourselves, by personalities and scandal and the news cycle, that we aren't paying attention to the fact that Earth's biological systems are collapsing as the planet heats up. At some point, books just won't matter. We'll all be forced to do what we evolved to do: hunt for shelter, sex, clean water, and food."

"Damn it," I said.

"You know what?" Scott said. "Let's not go on too long about any of this. We're here to see the monster. I don't really like to talk too much about this stuff anyway because there isn't that much interesting shit to say about it."

Scott and I stared into the murky distance across the lake to see nothing but the rippling waters pushed into shore on a light wind. Some

We stared into the murky distance to see the rippling waters pushed into shore.

say the lake is dead, that the massive hydroelectric project in the eastern highlands (built 2002-2006) serving Alcoa's great aluminum smelter downstream has dramatically increased the water's turbidity, killing off aquatic vegetation, fish, and bird life. Later I would meet up with a painter, Johanna Bogadóttir, in Reykjavík. In our far-ranging conversation over coffee, she told me that the current government of Iceland is not special in any way. They operate like every other government. They offer favors to wealthy businesses and businesspeople, and they extract resources from the earth for profit, leaving behind poisons and pollution and environmental wreckage for the future to clean up. "The government focuses on projects that profit the wealthy, and it cuts programs for the people, education and public works," she told me. "People here are as angry as in other places." On the surface, Iceland appears to be the world as it once was—clean water and air, abundant wildlife, a sustainable human population—a place where, as Darwin writes at the end of *The Origin of Species*, "endless forms most beautiful and most wonderful have been, and are being, evolved." Turns out no place on earth is safe from the appetites of nations. How can such a monster survive without clean water, without aquatic vegetation, without the fish and birds? How can we?

"I think I see the monster," I said. "Out in those little waves."

"I'm sure you do," Scott said. "Here, have another. Let's finish this bottle."

The story of the monster's origin first appeared in print in Icelandic writer Jón Árnason's two-volume collection *Icelandic Folktales and Legends* (1862, 1864) and is retold in Jacqueline Simpson's 1972 book by the same title. It goes like this: long ago, a woman living near the lake gave her daughter a gold ring and told her to place it beneath a baby lyngorm, a mythical dragonlike creature that reportedly loves gold.[27] As the lyngorm grows, she told her daughter, the gold ring will make more gold and make you rich. The girl did as she was instructed, placing the ring beneath a tiny lyngorm in a box. Days later she discovered that the lyngorm had grown so large, the box had split open. Frightened, she threw it into the lake, lyngorm, gold, and all. Set free, the beast grew into a great monster and terrorized the local farms and towns. Two men from Finland (apparently good at such things) were called in to destroy it and succeeded only in fettering it to the bottom of the lake. Rendered mostly harmless, Largarfljótsormurinn rises above the waves now and again, and the sight of it is a sign of bad things to come: foul weather, failed crops, a visit from the mother-in-law.

Either that story is true or this next one is, as suggested by twentieth-century American writer Avram Davidson. Davidson asks us to note the parallel between the words *lyngorm* and "long-worm," and the correspondence between those two words with the word *lingam*, Sanskrit for the male energy through the phallus. Instead of a literal reading of the story (girl catches a small monster that becomes a big one), try Davidson's figurative reading: young woman meets a man who develops an erection (long-worm) and then loses her virginity (splitting box), which, naturally, frightens her. Then there is all the water imagery, which likely means the woman conceived and bore a child. Choose one story or both.

Drinking rum and waiting for the monster, Scott and I came to know one of the greatest pleasures of foreign travel: idleness, the unfettered freedom to do whatever, wherever, and whenever we wished. The only struggle we had was that we are both industrious people. Imagine how we suffered doing nothing at all, and in doing nothing, finding nothing more that needed doing.

"Maybe we're wasting our time," I finally said, "sitting here and doing nothing."

"We're not doing nothing," Scott said. "We're drinking this rum. We're having a conversation. We're looking at this nice lake. We're waiting for the monster."

"So we are," I said.

"And it's a fine and ordinary thing to do."

"In an exotic place," I added.

"Or an ordinary place," Scott said. "At least it's ordinary to the people who live here."

He was right, of course, and yet Iceland's image as exotic has persisted since Viking settlement a thousand years ago. By the fifteenth and sixteenth centuries, Europeans had come to believe that the laws of physics operated differently here, that the plants and animals could be found nowhere else on earth, that Mount Hekla housed the door to hell, that Iceland, in fact, is hell. In her fine book *Iceland Imagined*, Karen Oslund writes that early travelers brought back reports of "an isolated place remote from the centers of civilization, covered with ice and fire, shrouded in clouds of poisonous smoke, the inhabitants like doomed souls, begging for relief." Early maps pictured Iceland swarming with monsters, and even into modern times the huldufólk, or hidden people, are a force in people's lives, evidenced by reports that the group Friends of Lava opposed a recent road project near Reykjavík by raising concerns about the impact on elvish culture.[28] The eruption of the Laki volcano in 1783 (and Hekla in 1845) enforced these perceptions, as it drove a famine that killed 20 percent of the population. Such bad press only encourages travelers and adventure seekers who, in their enthusiasm for the fantastic, come to Iceland for its perceived dangers and rarified beauty, its supernatural beings and monsters.

Auden, too, embraced Iceland as a land of smoke and monsters and wrote extensively about Shakespeare's great island drama, *The Tempest*. Cast away on a remote island, the play's protagonist, Prospero, wields immense magical power, but he and his daughter, Miranda, are cut off from the warmth and stability of society. He desires most to escape the island and return home to Milan, despite the fact that to do so he must break his staff and drown his book (the source of his power), only to face old age and death. The universal opposites of good and evil, spirit and body, freedom and imprisonment are separated into two characters on the island, just as the island itself embodies both characters: Ariel, a sprite of the air; and Caliban, a half-fish, half-man of the earth, a "thing of darkness," as Prospero calls him.[29] The image of the island, Auden writes in *The Enchafèd Flood*, "has two possibilities. Either it is the real earthly paradise, in which case it is a place of temporary refreshment for the exhausted hero, a foretaste of rewards to come . . . or it is . . . an illusion caused by black magic to tempt the hero to abandon his quest, and which, when the spell is broken, is seen to be really the desert of barren rock, or a place of horror." Islands, then, are testing grounds for heroic travelers who, in conquering the monsters of an otherworldly place, are also conquering the inferior part of themselves to reach a deeper level of self-awareness. Islands force hero-travelers to grow up.

These images of Iceland, ranging from earthly paradise to dark horror, did not encourage membership in a world of modernizing nations, and so, according to Oslund, during the Enlightenment, Danish and Icelandic writers "attempted to use their position of authority and privileged knowledge about Iceland . . . to counter . . . romantic and wild claims." They worked hard to transform the image of their country into a more ordinary place. And an ordinary place Iceland is. Turns out, the laws of physics still hold here, Icelandic plant and animal species occur elsewhere in the world, and it is highly unlikely that Mount Hekla is in fact the door to Hell. Moreover, talk about modernizing: Iceland boasts one of the world's highest literacy rates,[30] is considered one of the world's most gender-equal countries, and offers free Wi-Fi almost everywhere. The wrench in such progress is progress. Tourism has become the country's number one industry,[31] and travelers perpetuate Iceland's exotic image by mad endeavors like sitting near a lake and waiting for a monster.

"Well," I said. "I don't think the monster is going to show."

"Probably not," Scott said.

"The temperature is dropping too. Or maybe it's just that the wind is coming up."

"Here," Scott said, pouring out the last of the rum. "This will warm you up. Let's wait a bit longer."

When I go into wild places, my senses come alive, tuned to the earth and air, to the smallest sound or sign of something's presence or something passing. Though I have never seen a monster, I have always trusted that there are more things in heaven and earth than I might imagine. Here, staring at the lake, I held on to the hope that the monster would appear and prove to me that the universe we live in is deeper and wider than did ever plummet sound. I looked hard at the jiggling waters, hoping for some light from the darkness. I had been imagining this moment for more than a year, imagining Iceland's eastern fjords and lakes, this lake and its monster. Waiting for a monster is a bit like waiting for a messiah who will lead you to a promised land. It's a noble pursuit for the faithful, but you risk living out your life in limbo. Maybe the trick is to be ready for the monster or the messiah but to lead yourself instead.

I stood up.

"Ready?" Scott said.

"Yeah," I said, draining my cup.

Walking back into town, Scott stopped dead in his tracks.

"Shit, man," he said. "There's the monster."

Sure enough, there along the long white wall of the Netto discount grocery was a painted black form of the monster, head pointed to the left, tail on the right. It had no eyes or fins or distinctions of any kind, just a long, wavy, black form, like a Rorschach.

"That's her," Scott said.

"Yeah," I said. "The monster has appeared."

The next morning we returned to the Valney Café, where the day before we drank what we proclaimed was the best coffee in Iceland. The front door was open, so we walked in. The old woman, master and commander of the place, sat at a table hunched over a bowl of something. She raised her head like a moose from a bog and scowled at us. "No," she said, and moved to chase us out the door.

We walked around to the back and sat on a public bench to wait for the place to open. "The Wi-Fi is on," Scott said. "We can at least read our email and such until she's ready for us inside."

Just as we began to do so, the signal blinked out.

"Aw, man," Scott said. "She turned it off."

"What?"

"Yeah. She pulled the plug."

We looked up to see her moosey face in the window, the dark circles of her penetrating eyes, her mouth moving into a wind-battered scowl.

"The east is failing," Scott said.

An hour later we got on a bus headed south to Höfn.

Let's Take the Bus, Part Three
The Mariner
FROM EGILSSTAÐIR TO HÖFN, AND HÖFN TO REYKJAVÍK

"Welcome, gentlemen. Welcome to my bus," the driver said as we boarded in Höfn. "Do you know where you are going? And do you know from where you have come? These are philosophical questions, of course. You have come from the east? You have never drove this road before? You will see a beautiful country. So very beautiful you will want to drop everything and live here forever."

He shook our hands as we stepped up, his eyes like illuminated glass. "Please," he said. "Sit where you please. It will just be a moment before we are off into these beautiful lands."

Clear skies on that brilliant morning in Höfn, a small town on the eastern shore famous for its lobster. The town sits on a spit of land extending into a bay braced by barrier islands with an outlet to the sea. We took breakfast and coffee sitting in front of the tent where we had slept, a night lulled by an eerie washing sound reverberating against the backdrop mountains, on top of which you could see the great white mass of Vatnajökull. We were packed, ready to catch the morning bus to Reykjavík.

On our walk to the bus stop, I identified two birds I had been seeing for some days—the whimbrel (*Numenius phaeopus*), a wide-ranging shorebird with a distinctive long-hooked beak it uses to probe the sand for invertebrates; and the black-headed gull (*Chroicocephalus ridibundus*), a relatively small bird that, like most gulls, eats nearly anything, and whose eggs, when hardboiled, are prized in Britain.

"In Reykjavík, the people are crying," our driver said as we sat down. "They are crying on such a glorious day as this in Höfn. You see, when the weather is fine in Höfn, it is bad in Reykjavík, where all the people live. So they are crying. And how did you gentlemen sleep last night? Soundly? Or were you disturbed by the echo of the sea? I am sure you understand what I mean. When the temperature is right, about one degree Celsius as it was last night, with clear skies, we get the echo of the sea from the mountains. It is as the sound of machinery at work all night. Nature's machinery! Some people find it too strange, and they have trouble sleeping. But to me it is a balm, the sound of my home, Höfn, the most beautiful place in all of Iceland. Maybe in all the world."

Our driver was an average-sized fellow with full dark hair and a kind face with penetrating blue eyes, not penetrating because they were blue but for the way he fixed you in his gaze, a clear-eyed, wondering gaze, very much alive. You could see right away that he lived with certainty about the depth and meaning of his life, that life had come into alignment with his purpose and mission. He possessed a gentle ease that came from living as he was born to live, a man who knew who he was and where he was going. To be in our driver's presence was to come into the center of goodness and hope.

He had lived most of his life in Höfn, he told us, and when he was young went to work as a fisherman. At twenty-six, he became captain of his own boat. At age fifty, he retired. "All that time," he said, "full twenty-four years, I was at sea." He traded his boat for this bus, and he was now its captain, making the daily run from Höfn to Vík, from Vík back to Höfn, the road following the edge of the sea he once had roamed. Scott and I came to call him the Mariner.

"The hurricanes that pass Cuba and come up the east coast of America," he said, "fourteen days after Cuba, they reach Iceland. Sometimes they pick up more energy from the coast of Greenland, then hit Iceland hard. The wind can be very strong, maybe seventy meters a second, and when it is that strong it tears the asphalt off the roads."

Scott and I blinked in wonderment.

"So the Iceland house is built very strong to stand such winds. And, of course, you are wondering about the waves on the sea in that kind of wind. Yes, they are very high on the sea. Eight or nine meters. We have a system of measuring devices positioned along the coast so anyone with a TV or a computer can get the wave height data. The largest wave recorded was nineteen meters high."

We blinked again in astonishment.

"When the waves are high, the sea is very beautiful," the Mariner said. "The sea in its fury is very beautiful. I know. I have spent half my life at sea."

Just then a young fellow boarded the bus.

"Welcome, gentleman," the Mariner said. "Welcome to my bus. Where are you going? And where are you from? Do you know? These are philosophical questions. If you have never drove this road before, you will see a beautiful country. So very beautiful you will want to drop every-thing and live here forever."

"Cheers, mate," the fellow said.

"And cheers to you," the Mariner said.

"Hello, fellas," the fellow said to us.

A Kiwi, clearly, who told us he had been hill walking alone at the foot of the glacier these past five days. Before that he was in Belgium racing bikes (it was unclear if he meant cycling or motorcycling), and he thought he might as well stop off in Iceland to see the sights on his way home. "I probably shouldn't have been out there in the hills alone. But I was, and I loved it. I made some pretty sketchy traverses, and at one point thought I'd gotten myself into a real fix. But here I am now, and headed to the Westman Islands. How are you fellas getting on?"

We told him fine, fine, just fine.

"Awe-right," he said. "Say, Icelandic? What a language, eh? What a work-out. It's impossible to pronounce anything, especially these place-names."[32]

"Icelandic pronunciation is very easy," the Mariner said.

And since he had our attention: "Let me tell you something, gentle-men. The people in Höfn, they do not want too much. Not like Ameri-cans. We want only a good job, a place to live, food, and time with our family and friends. And that is all. It's not too much to ask. And so life here in Höfn is very simple, very easy, because we don't ask for too much. Yes, that's how it is," he said. "My time at this stop is ended, gentlemen. We will now travel through a very beautiful country. I will show you my land and my sea."

What the Mariner called his land and sea, this broad sweep of southern Iceland from Höfn to Reykjavík, was one of the country's last coasts to be settled. It has long been known as a region of violent and dangerous seas, harborless and plagued by heavy surf, a graveyard at the murky bottom scattered with the skeletons of men and ships. Norse people sailed wide of this coast to catch the Gulf Stream northward and find safer harbors on the country's west coast, including the city now known as Reykjavík.

Our bus pulled out, the Mariner at the wheel, steady, confident, wide awake.

"Look around you. Have you been traveling in a lot of rain this sum-mer? Today is fine in Höfn, but this has been a cold and rainy summer, and usually in summer we enjoy drier and more pleasant days. But this summer has been very rainy, very dark. But it is also good. The flowers and the grasses, they like this weather very much."

Our road took us inland along the great fan of a drainage leading from the glacier to the sea, until it narrowed enough to make a bridge possible. We crossed there and turned southwest. The glacier grew over our heads, a massive white topping on the cake of the land.

"This section of highway, part of what we call the Ring Road, was not built for travelers and tourists," the Mariner said. "It was built so farmers could move from place to place. It was paved completely only ten years ago and consists of many narrow bridges over many rivers flowing from the glacier. From 1960 to 1970, the construction of the road from Höfn to Vík was underway. In those days the road opened to traffic only on Tuesdays. There is no other road from here to there, so you could only go on Tuesdays. And if the weather was bad, then the road remained closed, and it would open again the next Tuesday. It would not open on Wednesday or Thursday when the weather cleared. Why should they change their schedule because the weather was bad? If you live in Iceland, if you are accustomed to these conditions, then a Tuesday road is no problem for anyone."

He paused and looked into his mirror to see that we were listening.

"I don't know how much you like history," the Mariner said. "But I cannot stop talking."

We crossed the bridge at Jökulsárlón, one of Iceland's most famous tourist destinations, and turned into the parking lot.

"We will make a brief stop here, gentlemen," the Mariner said. "Please step out and have a look at the iceberg lagoon. I bet you have not seen such things where you are from? You will see here the many luminous blue icebergs. Very beautiful. Very haunting. Up the road a bit, the sea has reclaimed three hundred feet of the shoreline. Quite suddenly. We need another good volcanic eruption to put the land back. And we will surely get it," he said. "Here at Jökulsárlón the glacier is retreating, and when it is gone the fjord now beneath it will be thirty-one kilometers long. Now the sea comes into the little bay with these icebergs to work at the edge of the glacier. Six hours in. Six hours out with the tide. For as long as the days of the sun.

"Also, gentlemen, perhaps you know of a man called James Bond? 007? The fifteen-minute opening of *A View to a Kill* was filmed here and released in 1985. It cost thirty-five million euros and two months to make the fifteen minutes. Surely I am exaggerating. And in that scene, you will see Bond, played by Mr. Roger Moore, skiing down a mountain to escape the Russian bad guys. Iceland as Russia! But, gentlemen, do you see a mountain to ski down? No, you do not. There is no mountain

"I bet you have not seen such things where you are from?"

here for skiing down, though Mr. Bond is a very good skier. I have to tell you also that I do not care for the new James Bond. I do not care for the technical movie of today. I prefer the James Bond of Sean Connery and Roger Moore, because, you see, I like how they touch the woman. I prefer a more erogenous James Bond. Well, gentlemen, our time here has ended. Shall we continue on our journey?"

As we were about to pull onto the highway, a middle-aged German cyclist approached the door of the bus.

"May I get on here?" the cyclist asked. "I want to go only a little way down the road. I have a route to cycle, but I want to skip this next part. Will you put my bike in the cargo bay beneath the bus?"

"Yes, certainly it is okay," the Mariner said. "I will take you. But please, just put the bike there yourself because today I am much too lazy."

We traveled on, and the storm blast came, chasing us south and west along the sea. It grew wondrous cold, and the sea became green as emerald, covered over in a dismal sheen. This was the rain and blow that were making the people cry in Reykjavík, and the closer we came to the city, the deeper we penetrated the storm.

"You see this landscape," the Mariner said, as we tunneled down the road. "It was made by a great bulldozer." He pointed up at the glacier. "The glacier was much nearer to the sea 120 years ago, but it is now retreating. I am told that these are the highest glacier waves in the world. Here is the bulldozer's work, where the land is made into these great hills, one after another, like waves. The glacier pushed and pulled and pushed and left the earth like this. Isn't it very beautiful?"

We crossed a bridge spanning a vast alluvial fan of black volcanic rock and sand. I later identified this place on my map as Skeiðarársandur.

"This is the longest bridge in Iceland," the Mariner said. "But there is no river here anymore. This flat plain was made by a great flood that broke out from the glacier when an eruption shook the ground in 1996. For a few hours, a river flowed out of the glacier that was wider than the Amazon."

We crossed another bridge spanning another great plain of black volcanic sand. "Here there was another flood," the Mariner said. "Look down below. You see there poking up out of the sand? There is the memory of the old bridge that was destroyed so suddenly."

We crossed yet another bridge. "We are crossing a bridge made of wood," he told us. "This is the third bridge in this location. It is a temporary bridge while they work on the permanent bridge. You see, Iceland is a land that makes and remakes itself again. And then again. How beautiful!"

At the crossroads leading up to Landmannalaugar, the landscape made famous by the claim that Tolkien used it as a model for his Middle Earth, we stopped so the German could get off.

"I am happy I was able to catch your bus," the German said. "Three years ago I cycled this route, but I didn't remember how far it was from Jökulsárlón to here. It was much longer than I remember."

"Yes," the Mariner said, nodding his head. "Sometimes we have a goldfish memory."

We traveled on into the storm, farther and farther away from the brilliant skies of Höfn, the storm wrapping the fog of cloud behind us like a following bird. We arrived at Vík in a heavy downpour. The Mariner stood to address us.

"Gentlemen. I hope you have enjoyed traveling through my beautiful country. And I hope you have learned something during your journey. Now you must change to another bus for Reykjavík. I will return along the sea road to my home in Höfn, where the sun is shining." He smiled. "I bid you a good life. Thank you. And so long."

Scott and I stepped off into the rain, and the bus to Reykjavík pulled in right away. We queued up at the door with a dozen other people. We waited, the rain battering and soaking us. The door finally opened to a man with an angry face who was so big he filled the passageway. Our new driver. We stepped aside to let him out so that we could all get on, but he closed the bus doors, locked them, and walked into the station.

"Well," I said to Scott. "From here, it's going to be a different kind of ride."

"Yup," Scott said. "And for this new driver, compared to the Mariner, it's going to be a different kind of life."

A Visit to the World's Only Penis Museum
AROUND REYKJAVÍK

nside a small wooden box on the wall at the Icelandic Phallological Museum in Reykjavík are fifteen silver penises, sculptures honoring Iceland's 2008 Olympic silver medal-winning handball team. Handball is a national obsession here, and the players who brought back the silver are national heroes. A photograph of the team is featured above the box, and one immediately associates the position of the players with the position of the members. Alas, there is no such fun in it, as the sculptor, Þorgerður Sigurðardóttir, daughter of museum founder Sigurður Hjartarson, made the penises to honor the team, but the team had nothing to do with the penises. They did not pose for the sculptor. She sculpted, so she has said, from her own experience.

At the museum, located on a quiet street not far from the Argentina Steakhouse, you are greeted at the door by large beach stones placed to look like a monstrous cock and balls.[33] The museum houses a collection of more than two hundred mammal penises and parts, the largest of which is the sperm whale and the smallest the wee hamster, which requires a magnifying glass to see, and even then it's not clear what you are looking at. The penis of almost every mammal in Iceland is represented, including *Homo sapiens sapiens*, along with a number of mammal penises from other parts of the world. Some are preserved in jars of formalin, and others poke out from the wall, like the bull elephant penis, which looks like a tree root, the skin of which is thick and rough like bark.

A brief history. Hjartarson, the museum's founder, spent his boyhood on a farm where he used a bull's pizzle as a whip to control livestock. Years later, a friend gave him a bull's pizzle to poke fun at his rural upbringing, and soon others gifted him penises from other mammals. The collection grew, and after Hjartarson retired in 2004 from thirty-seven years as a teacher and school principal, he opened the museum in Húsavík in northern Iceland, a small town known for whale watching. Hjartarson's son, Hjörtur Gísli Sigurðsson, took over as curator in 2011 and moved the museum to Reykjavík, where about two-thirds of Icelandic people live and most tourists visit.

Walking through this museum is a bit like shopping in a medieval apothecary but with more lighting. You move carefully around the rooms looking over the specimens on the walls, while behind you are dazzling displays of phalluses preserved in glass tubes, some rising to the height of a man—whales, of course. What you see floating in those tubes is otherworldly, often pale, bent, and twisted fleshy forms, like a house of alien worms. The space itself is immaculate: a clean, blue-tinged carpet, which reminded me of the sea; a tidy gift shop, with my favorite item for sale, a penis cheese cutter; and a well-ordered installation of specimens. I felt a kind of fastidiousness at work. While I was there, the blonde-haired woman from the front desk moved about the museum, dusting the penises with a cloth. I detected nothing odd or overtly self-conscious about her actions. She offered a platonic smile as if she were cleaning glassware or fine crystal.

I did not meet the museum's founder but viewed a few photographs of him, through which one might get a sense of his character. In one he stands commandingly, his feet shoulder-width apart, dressed in navy-blue polyester pants and a matching vest over an ivory-colored, short-sleeved shirt. His face is rectangular but soft, like his middle; a quiet and thoughtful-looking man. I thought of him as a hybrid of two great American TV personalities, Mr. Green Jeans and Captain Kangaroo. In

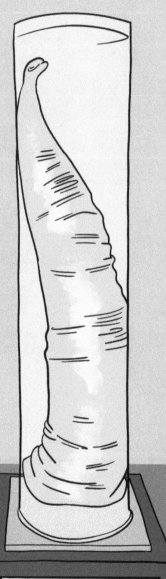

What you see floating in those tubes is otherworldly, like a house of alien worms.

Sperm Whale Penis

the second photograph, Hjartarson wears a burgundy button-up sweater, the kind of garment suited to older gentlemen. His face is drawn down, and he stares into a distant foreground talking on a telephone, the handset of which is a carved wooden penis. It's the kind of photograph that might incite laughter, but something about Hjartarson lets you know the museum is no joke. This is a serious collection for serious study, despite the fact that many visitors wander about concealing a modest smirk behind a raised hand.

As I stood before the penises of the handball team, I overheard two young women across the way.

"Oh, my god," one said, and gasped. "Is that . . . it iiizzz!"

"Is it?" the other said. "Oh, my god. It's human. And those are the balls."

"Really. Man balls? I can't believe it."

"Oh," the other said, flehming her lips. "I'm so glad I'm not having sex tonight. I don't think I could."

"I can't look at it any longer," said the first. "Let's go."

But they didn't go. They lingered in silence, staring at the dick in the jar.

The dick in the jar belonged to a ninety-five-year-old Icelander, Páll Arason, who pledged in 1996 to donate his parts when he died, which he did in 2011. When I visited, the museum's collection included two other human specimens: the foreskin of a forty-year-old Icelander and the testicles and epididymis of a sixty-year-old Icelander. Preserved in a jar, the human male genitals are not all that impressive. Arason's signature parts look more like a hairy blob than the impressive staff you might see on a male porn star anywhere on the internet.

As a regular guy, with modestly irregular appetites, I wondered what the female genitals might look like so removed and preserved in a jar. Strange that what is so gloriously fascinating and desirable in life can be rather revolting in death. Who out there will be the first to open a companion museum across the street lovingly devoted to exploration and elevation of the vagina?

Until Arason died, a human specimen was the one mammal penis missing from the collection. The museum was in hot pursuit, and several men wrote letters of donation (now on display at the museum), each vying for the honor of being the first. One, American Tom Mitchell, announced that he would have his cock surgically removed while he was still alive. He regarded his member as a living entity separate from himself, an entity he named Elmo. Once detached, Elmo, who wears a tattoo of the red, white, and blue across his head, would become the most famous dick in the world. A Canadian documentary film, *The Final Member*, tells Mitchell's story. When I asked Sigurðsson, the new museum curator, if Mitchell had fulfilled his promise, he said, "No. He is still talking about having it done, but I don't think he will go through with it."

Despite the sad ugliness of Arason's member in that jar, when attached and fully functional the average human male has the biggest dick in the primate world. The gorilla averages only one and a quarter inches. The orangutan, one and a half inches. The chimpanzee, three inches. The human male, a full five inches on average. Why are humans so endowed compared to other primates? Jared Diamond, in *The Third Chimpanzee*, reports that the human penis is a display feature like a peacock's tail. Not a display feature for women, who report they are more aroused (at least initially) by other features like legs, shoulders, the voice, perhaps a kind smile. The penis is a display feature to impress and intimidate other men. Arguably, men are at least as obsessed with the penis as women are and care a great deal about its size. Most men who have spent any time in a locker room understand the urge to have a look around and see how they compare: big man, average man, wee man. And yet, curiously, 60 percent of visitors to this museum are women.

Moving through the museum, I found the object of my personal fascination. Arranged on a shelf behind glass, a bit slapdash, it seemed to me, was a display of bacula, or penis bones, from several marine mammals—seals mostly and a couple of walruses.

Years ago I saw a penis bone for the first time in the hatband of a friend. Cory and his wife, Sunny, lived on forty acres inherited from his family. They had a bit of everything: sheep, llamas, a wood-fired kiln, a wind generator, a backhoe (Cory was possibly the best backhoe operator in Northern California), a mobile sawmill, and the penis bone. Until I looked at Cory's hat and asked, "What's that," I didn't know that most mammals have a penis bone. I knew I didn't have a penis bone. But come to find out, raccoons have a penis bone, coyotes, badgers, most carnivores, most rodents (not rabbits, for some reason), and even most bats. And primates too. But not humans. And not spider monkeys. Or hyenas.

The raccoon baculum in Cory's hat was elegant to look at, a graceful S curve, though not dramatic, perhaps more like a J, the hook of which is proximal, and the subtle swoop, distal. The baculum is not anchored at another bone but floats in the tissue of the penis like battens in a sail. I was drawn to it right away, and I wanted one for my own hat. I settled for the rib of a fish I found on a canoe trip on the Rio Grande, and when people asked about it I lied and said it was a penis bone. With this admission, I can't get away with that anymore, but I won't have to. I discovered recently that I can buy a baculum of my own from the Evolution Store. A raccoon goes for ten dollars, and I can get a set of four (raccoon, coyote, fox, mink) for thirty-nine dollars.

The baculum does what you think it does: it helps maintain stiffness during sex, not unlike the penile implants that help correct erectile dysfunction. I guess those work pretty well—I know a poet who has one and uses it all the time. He refers to it affectionately as his "automatic cock." The word *baculum* finds its root in the Latin for "cudgel" or "stick," and even "scepter."[34] Cudgel may sound silly when thinking of these small animals, but the walrus baculum is nearly two feet long and looks like the oaken tire knockers you find for sale at truck stops. I stared and wondered, *What would it be like to pack that thing in your shorts?*

The baculum is old, evolutionarily speaking, and the fact that humans have lost it is an interesting side note. The human erection works by fluid dynamics and requires good circulation and blood pressure. A weak erection can be a sign of illness or disease, emotional problems like excessive stress or depression, and thus a sign of weak genes. As the baculum can disguise a weak erection, without it, the human male is left with his vigor, or lack of it, on display. If you are a woman looking for a baby daddy, you will have healthier, more successful children with a man who has an impressive erection.

Deeper in mythical time, you've probably heard the story that God made Eve from Adam's rib. Yet, astonishingly, human males are not missing a rib. What bone are human males missing? Right. Some scholars believe that God removed Adam's baculum to make Eve. I'm not making this up. Consider that the Hebrew word *tzela*, which has been translated as "rib" in most editions of the Bible, also means "structural support beam." Also note that in Genesis, God closes up the wound he makes in Adam to make Eve, but there is no mark or scar along the ribs. Look down, and you'll find a distinct seam or suture called the "raphe" right down the middle of every man's cock and balls.

Also from Genesis (the Robert Alter translation, which is superior), when Eve is presented to Adam, he says: "This one at last, bone of my bones / and flesh of my flesh / This one shall be called Woman, / for from Man was this one taken." The "one at last" that was taken from Man is certainly Woman, but it is also the one bone, which must be the baculum, the only bone important enough to a man to call the "bone of my bones." It makes good sense, then, that the word "bone" has come to mean an erect penis. As further proof, just imagine you are sitting at a bar and a woman you are immediately attracted to walks up. You turn to her and say, "I would like to share with you the bone of my bones." I'm nearly certain she won't think you are talking about your favorite rib. Giving up the baculum to create women was a major sacrifice for men, and thus far we have received very little credit for it.

One more point to bring this wonderful museum into focus. Most travelers in Iceland will happen upon stories about huldufólk, or hidden people, in which some Icelanders reportedly believe. In a small room at the back of the museum you'll find the folklore collection. Here are the penises and parts of various fantastic creatures that wander back and forth between the world we know and the world we don't know. Included are the pricks of an Icelandic elf preserved in "pure Arctic water," a troll (*Homo gigantus islandicus*), a water horse, a merman, a sea howler (a kind of sea monster), Þorgeir's Bull, the baculum of an enriching beach mouse (which pulls money from the sea for its owner), and the shrunken testicles of the corpse-eating cat of Thingmúli.

It's difficult to know how to come to terms with Iceland's phallological museum. It's a bit overwhelming, really. I walked about with my camera trying to document the madness of it, the scariness of it, the utter amazement of a whale dork as big as a man. At first I regarded the place as a novelty, a playful game for tourists. Later I began to see that serious study could take place here, but to what end? What might we gain from focused study of mammal penises? Could such a facility be useful in studying testicular and prostate cancers, and erectile dysfunction in other mammals? Are these primarily problems in humans, or are they also problems for marsupial mice? What is the relationship between such cancers and the quality of our air, our water, our diet? I learned recently that the bonobo, our closest primate relative, is vegetarian and doesn't get prostate cancer. Can a museum like this help us cure and prevent such diseases? Or perhaps the benefits are social: greater understanding of ourselves might be achieved by looking closely at the male organ most cultures keep mostly hidden. Then another thought became clear as I exited through the gift shop: as much as we know about our world, there is always more to discover. The capacity of the earth to excite and amaze—let us state it freely—is boundless.

The Troll Wife's Mountain and Other Stories

REYKJAVÍK TO ÞINGVELLIR TO REYKJAVÍK

After Scott left Iceland and I was alone and adrift, I came to understand that I needed to make a journey deeper into the interior, into the highlands, at least as far in as Þingvellir, the country's most famed national park and a UNESCO World Heritage site, where early Icelanders (despite their modern reputation as lawless Vikings) established the world's first and longest-running democratic parliament, the Alþingi, in AD 930.

The highlands is a country without animals, as animals live mostly at the country's periphery—marine mammals, fish, birds. The arctic fox has always been here, but the rats and cats and mink, the sheep and horses and caribou, came to Iceland with people. A vast deserted land of rock and fire, the highlands became fixed in my mind when I learned that the region has long been a refuge for outlaws, thieves, despots, and no-good hooligans. It is also one of the few remaining refuges in all the world for trolls.

If you do that thing where you fly to Europe on Icelandic Air and touch down in Reykjavík for a night or two en route, you do one or two or three of three things: you go to the Blue Lagoon for a soak and maybe dinner; you tour the city on foot, visit museums and buildings, drink beer and eat puffin; and you go to Þingvellir. As I was hanging around in

The highlands is a country without animals.

Reykjavík awaiting permission to visit the Árni Magnússon Institute to look at some really old books, I determined that getting out of town for a daylong bus tour of the Golden Circle was an excellent way to pass the time. The Golden Circle is comprised of three main points of interest: Geysir, apparently the very geyser from which the word "geyser" originated; Gulfoss, perhaps Iceland's best-known waterfall, no doubt due to its proximity to Reykjavík as well as its beauty; and Þingvellir.

I had rented a basement room in a private home east of the city center,[35] so it was a bit of a walk along the seawall to Harpa concert hall where I would board a bus for the tour. Passing the *Sun Voyager* yet again, I noticed a fellow standing still and facing the sea, gazing longingly onto those grayish waters under the overcast morning sky, his shirt pulled off and held in his hand. The walking path was quiet but for a few joggers and cyclists, which was the usual pace of things. As I came by, the fellow raised his clenched fist and bellowed like a bull giving birth, altogether an unnatural sound since bulls don't give birth. I passed by unnoticed. Farther on I found a small red starfish cast onto the pavement as if the sea had spit it out. I picked it up. It looked alive to me, its underside still soft and tentacled, the hard g-spot roughness of its red back a surprise in my hand. What was there to do but toss it back in? No sooner did the starfish hit the water, splosh, but the sky spoke and it began to rain. The strangeness of these three events—the bellowing man, the starfish, the rain—caused me to think of them as braided threads in my story, knotted and fixed somehow to events yet to come.

At Harpa, I met my driver, Jón, who told me he worked as a guide only in the summer. His primary work was with the minister of welfare's office overseeing the Westfjords. When I told him about my walk in the Hornstrandir, he told me about his. We got on rather well.

I took a seat near the front of the bus, and with fewer than a dozen people, off we went east on Highway 1. Not far out of town we sped by a house hidden up in the trees. Jón felt compelled to explain, as he likely had numerous times on so many tours before, that behind the house was a cave where long ago a woman lived with her husband. When the woman was ready to give birth, her husband mounted his horse and road into town to fetch the midwife, and by the time he returned the baby had been born. The wife reported that a midwife had appeared and helped her with the birth. Impossible, said the midwife who arrived with the husband, as she was the only midwife in these parts. The couple came to understand that help had come from the huldufólk, and that help would be offered henceforth to whoever dwelled in that house.

"Fantastic story," I said to Jón. "So, I've heard that most Icelanders really do believe in hidden people. Is that true?"

"This is the question I get all day long from Americans," Jón said. "Let me explain it this way: the hidden people are Eve's unclean children. You see, Eve gave birth to clean children and unclean children. When God showed up to check on her, she hid her unclean children. He eventually found out because he is God, and now it's God who hides the unclean children from all of us."

"That doesn't help me much," I said.

"Just sit with it for a while," Jón said.

"Since we're on the subject," I said, "I understand that most Icelanders are descended from a small group of early settlers. And Auden says that Icelanders enjoy an uninhibited sex life, so you all use an app or an internet site or something to check relatedness and thus avoid incest. Is that true?"

Jón looked at me with annoyance and delight. "Oh, yes, it's true," he said. "When you meet a girl, it's really best to bump your phones together before you bump anything else."

Onward we went, crossing into the southern region of Iceland until we turned northward on Highway 35 and up the river Ölfusá to where it splits at Skálholt, then up the river Tungufljót to the waterfall Faxi, named after its likeness to the tails of Icelandic horses. The river makes a sharp bend there, turning the falls toward its outer bank, the water plunging and pooling at the bottom. That churning water looked like iron under the heavy, dark clouds of the day. The river is full of salmon, and Jón pointed out the salmon ladder around the falls. "Usually you build a salmon ladder to get the salmon around a human-made obstruction, like a dam," Jón said. "But in this case the locals wanted to get the salmon around this natural obstruction, which is Faxi, to allow more salmon upriver and sell more licenses for fishing. The world is a confusing place."

We all got back on the bus and pulled out of the parking lot. "Sheep alert!" Jón said. We all looked, and sure enough, a few sheep were crossing the road in front of us. "Sheep roam freely in Iceland," Jón told us, "and you don't want to hit sheep with your car. You must pay compensation to the farmer, and you will pay many times more than the value of the sheep. It is very expensive."

Back on the river Ölfusá, we stopped at Gulfoss, which falls in the shape of an arrow point onto a rocky bench, from which it falls again, the green and rocky canyon sprayed in fine mist. "Gulfoss has three things necessary for art," Jón said. "Power, beauty, and it is well placed. Now, while you look at the falls, let me tell you a story."

We all nodded.

A farmer's daughter lived on one side of Gulfoss, Jón told us, and a man lived on the other. The man fell in love with the young woman, as she was fair indeed. He shouted his proposal for marriage across the thundering falls. She was not impressed, nor interested in him, so she set up a challenge he would surely fail: if he could swim across the river she would marry him. The man, pricked by love, swam across the river, and the two were married. They had several beautiful children and lived happily ever after.

Some of the sweetest stories are not that interesting.

Back on the bus again, we ascended the mountains on what Jón identified as the Keel Road, so called because it was shaped like the keel of a ship. Where the road turned to gravel, we caught a glimpse of Langjökull, or Long Glacier, the second largest glacier in Iceland. It was dirtied by ash from the 2010 eruption of the volcano Eyjafjallajökull, the same eruption that disrupted air travel all over the world. A glacier lagoon from the river flows from Langjökull, and it is haunted by a beautiful Icelandic maiden. "Be careful," Jón warned us. "We have lost so many men who went out to find her. Sheep alert!" Jón said, pointing.

Deeper into the highlands, we stopped at a huge pyramid of stones. Looking out from the stone pile, Jón pointed out a crevice in the Blue Mountain where a rock giant once lived. The rock giant made a deal with a farmer, Jón told us. If the farmer would bury him when he died, the farmer would be rewarded with the rock giant's treasure. It came to pass that the rock giant did die, and the farmer journeyed to the rock giant's cave. Inside the cave, the farmer found a treasure chest. Upon opening it, he found only a bunch of dead leaves. He put a fistful of the leaves in his pocket (who knows why) and buried the giant's body. When the local church bells rang, the farmer noticed that his pocket had become very heavy. He reached into his pocket to discover that the leaves had turned to gold. He decided to return to the cave to get more leaves, but he could not find it. The cave had vanished.

"So, if you go looking, you won't easily find the rest of the rock giant's gold," Jón told us. "Nowadays, each traveler passing this point must toss a stone onto the pile for the rock giant. But toss your stone carefully. If your stone stays on the pile, you will have good luck. If your stone rolls off the pile, you will not have good luck. Now, please, honor the rock giant by adding a stone to the pile."

I selected a stone from the ground and tossed it up. It made a little bounce, then another, caught in a crevice, and stayed there.

Our journey went on this way, with Jón telling stories about what happened in the places we passed by. I recalled that in *Icelandic Folktales and Legends*, Jaqueline Simpson writes that "Icelandic stories are almost always firmly localized," that is, located in a specific place. I was reminded of traveling around central Idaho and northeast Oregon with Nez Perce elder Horace Axtell.[36] On the Snake River one day, Horace pointed out a place where Coyote used a fishnet to catch salmon, and he told that story. In Kamiah, Idaho, he pointed out a great stone mound that, he said, was the remains of a monster from which Coyote created all people, including the Nez Perce people, and he told that story. I asked Horace why he told the story of a place when we were passing through it. "Because the story lives in the place," he said. "It does not live in my mind. It lives outside in the land. So when we come into the place of the story, the story asks to be told."

Driving through Iceland's empty highlands, this interior desert, I asked Jón if he knew Jóhann Sigurjónsson's stage play *Eyvind of the Hills*, a retelling of the historical story of one of Iceland's most famous outlaws. "Oh, yes," Jón said. "It is a story about loneliness." And then he told Eyvind's story. A man named Eyvind, a fugitive thief, arrives in the north country of Iceland and hires on as a farm laborer. He falls in love with the rich widow who hired him, a woman named Halla. Halla's brother-in-law, a bailiff, is also in love with her. Attracted to his strength and character, Halla proposes marriage to Eyvind. The bailiff learns from others that

Eyvind is wanted by the law. He gathers his men and sets out to arrest Eyvind, thereby preventing the marriage and keeping Halla for himself. Alerted to this danger, Halla and Eyvind escape into the highlands, where they live happily for many years. They have a baby girl, Tota. A friend is with them, Arnes, who also falls in love with Halla. Halla rebukes him, and upon leaving his two friends he encounters the bailiff and a group of angry men searching for Eyvind. He runs back to warn Halla and Eyvind. Fearing capture, Halla casts her baby girl over a high cliff into a river torrent. Eyvind kills the bailiff with his knife and escapes with Halla deeper into the mountains to a small hut. As winter sets in, the couple runs out of food. They argue and fight in their hunger and weakness. They consider suicide to end their pain. One day Halla asks Eyvind to fetch more firewood. He does so, and while he is gone she wanders out into the snow and freezes to death. When Eyvind discovers Halla missing, he calls out for her, and then he too wanders into the snow to freeze to death. In the play's final scene, the audience watches as snow swirls and blows into the open door of the empty hut.

After Jón told that story, the small group of us on the bus sat there staring blankly at him. Jón stared blankly back at us. The sky darkened. Then Jón said, "Oh, another thing to remember is that the Holy Grail might be around here somewhere." He explained that a team of researchers under the direction of Italian cryptologist and archaeologist Giancarlo Gianazza has been coming to the highlands for many years to search for the grail. Gianazza has followed the stories in grail lore that mention the grail's secret location on an island, and he believes that island to be Iceland, and that the grail is somewhere in the highlands. "So, if you're roaming around out here and you find an old cup," Jón said, "it's probably the grail. Sheep alert!"

We drove the Kjölur Route across the vast and chunky Kjölur Plateau, windswept and dark, and northward between two great glaciers, to our east Hofsjökull and to our west Langjökull and the milky aqua lake it fills, Hvítárvatn. We turned east onto another gravel track to walk among the geothermal features at Kerlingarfjöll, a rhyolite mountain range of chalky and sulfurous colors venting from somewhere deep below. Jón called the mountain nearest to us Hex Mountain, which he said refers to hogs, or it refers to a bitchy woman (his words), or it refers to a great troll wife who lives in these parts.

In *Icelandic Folktales and Legends*, Simpson writes that Icelandic stories seek to explain natural features and phenomena. Strange rock formations are described as trolls turned to stone. "A few trolls are kindly," she writes, "but most are bad; most hate Christianity and have no religion of their own, though they are true to their promises." What is well documented in the country's laws and sagas is that "every part of the land had its guardian nature-spirits." These spirits lived inside stones, mountains, and other natural features. Trolls were "extremely displeased when Christianity began to spread through the land, and even more so when churches were built." Church bells can turn trolls to stone, and for this reason trolls often throw rocks at churches.

Jón led us along a trail that rose before it descended, and the sky became darker still, heavy with black clouds. You could hear the wind coming past your ears. "Even as we see so many vents and steam in this area," Jón said, "the next volcano to erupt in Iceland will be Mount Hekla, farther east, once known as the Gateway to Hell. It was predicted to erupt in 2010, but it didn't. Now we are all waiting." He shrugged and sighed. "Waiting for a volcano to erupt is like waiting for a pregnant woman to give birth."

Our small party walked the trail over the noses of a series of yellowed geothermal hills. We heard thunder crack overhead and saw lighting break. Like a bellowing man, thunder cracked again and again, and rain fell. Jón stopped us a moment. "We will be all right," he said. "We can complete our short walk. But this is very strange weather. Last night there was an immense storm here too, and the local people were afraid. So much thunder and lightning. We don't get this kind of weather in this area. I never imagined I'd be telling people to be aware of lightning in this place. Of course, by the time you are aware of lightning, it's already hit you. Maybe it's the troll wife. And I'm not really joking about that."

We hiked the trail to look into the geothermal pools and boils. Lightning flashed high overhead. On the ground I found a hard black material that had been ejected from the volcano and cooled very quickly. It looked nearly like obsidian.

"Look," Jón said, pointing. "This is the troll wife's mountain. Do you see the face of a woman? There, her face, and there, her breasts? Now you know about the troll, and so you also know about the hidden people. You look into the rocks, and you see their faces."

In Iceland, I kept stumbling onto stories of violent and predatory women, some of them trolls, who hunt and catch and carry off men for sex and marriage. Such women use men up, then kill them, and sometimes devour them. Halldór Laxness opens his novel *Independent People* with the story of Gudvor, "a woman of a most forceful nature, reputed to be skilled in occult lore and capable of changing her form." Her husband is described as a wretch who has "little freedom, being kept completely under her domination." The couple are not prosperous and cannot feed their children, so Gudvor forces her husband "to carry their newborn children out into the desert and leave them there to die." He lays them under flat rocks, and some he sinks into the lake, and if you travel in those lands, Laxness claims, "their wails may still be heard." Gudvor's husband vanishes from the story, and the local people understand that she murdered him, as she had murdered other men, "some for their possessions, others for their blood and marrow." The locals say that she kills guests she invites into her home by attacking them with "a short sword as they sleep, bites them in the throat and drinks their blood, then, after dismembering their bodies, uses their bones as playthings."

Among several such stories in Simpson's book is "How Kraka Lost Her Lover." The she-troll Kraka, who lived near Mývatn Lake, in northeast Iceland not far from Dettifoss, was "man-mad, and could not bear to live alone." She "got hold of a shepherd . . . whose name was Jón."[37] What becomes clear is that if Jón eats Kraka's food or has sex with her, he will turn into a troll himself and be forced to live in the frame of her life. Eventually she will likely kill and eat him. Jón must make a decision:

The she-troll Kraka was "man-mad, and could not bear to live alone."

relent and live in her frame, or live not at all. He resists and eventually tricks Kraka into going out to fetch him a twelve-year-old shark to eat, his favorite delicacy. In her absence he makes a run for it. Kraka pursues him, and as he reaches his homeland a farmer comes to his aid, threatening Kraka with a red-hot iron from the smithy's fire. Kraka retreats to her cave. It was a very close call.

On our way to Þingvellir we stopped at Geysir to watch it erupt, but it didn't. Apparently so many tourists have thrown rocks into the spout that the geyser is greatly diminished. Nearby, however, is Strokkur, known as the world's most reliable geyser. "Strokkur" means "churn," and the geyser erupts about every six minutes and shoots some sixty feet high or better, which it did.

Why are we attracted to such events, to geothermic water shooting out of the earth? Why do we prefer the moment of eruption to the interval between eruptions when the water far below is in the process of being superheated and preparing to come to the surface? Why do we prefer the brief moment of chaos and noise during an eruption, when clearly the quieter period before and after is superior, when the geyser has retreated into the earth, and you watch and listen to the steam and soft bubble, and gaze on the surrounding hills? Nature does not prefer one thing over another.

We traveled on and arrived quite suddenly at our final stop, Þingvellir, "assembly plains," the site of the Alþingi. In medieval times, the Alþingi was an annual June gathering to enact the country's business, where policy and laws were reviewed and agreed upon, cases heard and judged. Not only were chieftains and their entourages in attendance but also foreign dignitaries and heads of state, brewers and food sellers, sword sharpeners, peat cutters, tanners, merchants, traders, and laborers. Clowns and other entertainers came to perform, people came looking for work and sex and marriage partners, and beggars came to beg. Like all political gatherings, the Alþingi was a binge fest, a drinking party anchored by socializing and fornication. While the Alþingi has changed some over time, it survived union with Norway (1262), the Kalmar Union (1397), union with Denmark and Norway (1523), a move to Reykjavík (1844), home rule with Danish control (1918), and Icelandic sovereignty (1944). "All riding paths in Iceland once led to Þingvellir," Jón said.

Þingvellir is located in a rift valley, formed when the tensional forces of two tectonic plates—in this case, the North Atlantic Ridge—split the land apart and a block of land, called a graben, dropped between them. You get a steep-sided and relatively flat-bottomed depression or canyon, like the meridian trench Luke Skywalker flew into as he targeted the thermal exhaust port to destroy the Death Star. The valley is composed of a number of rift faults, the greatest of which are Almannagjá and Hrafnagjá. In this very place, Iceland is moving away from Europe. "Iceland is a young country in geological terms," writes Jónas Kristjánsson in *Iceland and Its Manuscripts*. "The North Atlantic Ridge broke the surface of the sea there during the last geological era, and it is still rumbling and unsettling, with the result that gaping holes open down into the earth and molten lava streams upwards."

Lakes are often associated with rift valleys, as Þingvellir is, located on the north shore of Þingvallavatn, the largest natural lake in Iceland. Þingvallavatn's exceptionally clear waters support three species of trout and cover 84 square kilometers at a maximum depth of 114 meters. By comparison, Lake Tahoe covers 490 square kilometers and has a maximum depth of 501 kilometers.

The sky came down and the rain came in, and I walked away from the group at Þingvellir. I dropped into Almannagjá, which Lord Dufferin calls "a black rampart," and while you cannot detect the movement of the plates, you have a clear sense that something is at work. It is apparent here that Iceland, and by extension the Earth, is remaking itself, just as the human body remakes its organs by replacing older and tired cells. You can feel the long extension of time and sense strange presences from the Alþingi a thousand years ago. This place serves to remind us that the Earth is even now changing, as it has since it coalesced out of the dust of interstellar space. We are all travelers in an antique land, sojourning on a planet that has a beginning, just as it will have an end.

We drove back to Reykjavík following a series of pipes, like the tentacles of a great sea beast running into the city—a geothermal plant, Jón said, that feeds the city with power and hot water. "Isn't it wonderful that our water comes hot right out of the ground? The supply is unlimited. You can take a hot shower for as long as you like. Sheep alert!"

When the bus pulled in at Harpa, I hopped off and, beneath a sky full of stars, hurried over to a bar called Home, a place where Scott and I had dined before. Upstairs from the dining room was the VIP gentlemen's club, but I had another kind of appetite. I ordered half a roasted chicken with all the sides and a beer, and, like a troll or an outlaw of the highlands, ate up the whole thing.

Behind the Doors of the
Árni Magnússon Institute
AROUND REYKJAVÍK

The trials and tribulations of books are equaled only by the trials and tribulations
of mankind; their sufferings are identical with those of their creators, and if they
live longer they are not immune from decay and death.
— Holbrook Jackson, *The Anatomy of Bibliomania*

O n my walk to the Árni Magnússon Institute, the research center and repository for Iceland's medieval manuscripts, a misty
fog blew in over the city. Morning mists descending from the
mountains, perhaps, or rising off the sea from the bays, maybe the breath-
stink of trolls. Flags snapped in the wind, and the air became more and
more viscous. I was walking inside a cloud. Making my way along the bay
shore, that great sculpture, the *Sun Voyager*, looked like a live thing ready
to break loose on sails and oars, and I thought I heard footsteps behind
me, a runner or someone walking fast, maybe Grendel. I turned to find
no one there.

Two thoughts came to me as I entered the city center and turned
onto Austurstræti Street, headed for a coffee at the Laundromat Café.
First, the world is not made more beautiful by more and more people, so
why are so many people so in love with making more people and not in
love with the world? Second, the allure of travel is based on what you, the

traveler, do not know, and what you cannot see ahead of you. If you knew what was coming, you would not go. While I marked those two thoughts down in my notes as important, I understood I'd think less of them in the morning.

My reasons for arranging a visit to the Árni Magnússon Institute arose from a general lifelong love of books and a curiosity about what made this country so imbued with book culture. Iceland is a nation of the book like none other. "Some nations have cities and cathedrals to remind people of their past," writes Vigdís Finnbogadóttir, former president of Iceland, in her preface to Kristjánsson's *Iceland and Its Manuscripts*, "we Icelanders have old manuscripts and books. . . . they represent the first enshrinement of the culture which still lives among us and thrives." If I take Finnbogadóttir at her word, along with what I came to understand during my time there, the idea that Iceland is a nation of the book is not an abstraction hidden in the minds of a handful of historians and cultural elites. It's alive in the people who walk Iceland's streets and fill the bars and farm the fields and fish the coastal waters, and I could not deny that I admired this about Icelanders and found it the very anchorage of beauty.

Admittance to the institute is usually reserved for students, researchers, and staff, and I was none of these. In advance of my journey, I set to work on arranging a visit merely as a curious writer. It took some doing, but eventually one of the librarians, Ólöf Benediktsdóttir, agreed to show me around.

When I arrived at the institute, blue sky was opening up, as if heaven had swallowed all that morning mist. It seemed like a good sign. I entered through the front doors of this rather unremarkable building and found another set of doors, huge wooden double doors locked tight like Hrothgar's mead hall after Grendel's rampaging. I rang the bell. No one answered. I rang the bell again. Still nothing. The third time I heard footsteps, and then the door opened a crack to a woman with short hair, professionally dressed, who was standing to block my way.

"What do you want?" the woman said.

"Good morning," I said cheerfully. "I'm here to see Ólöf. She is expecting me."

"Ólöf," she repeated.

"Yes. One of the librarians. I have an appointment with her."

"Ólöf," she said again. "What is your project?"

"My project?" I said, less cheerfully.

"Yes. Why are you here? What is your project? Do you not have a project?"

"Well, I'm a writer," I said, trying to sound official. "I guess most everything is a project."

She eyed me with suspicion. "I am a professor at the University of North Carolina, Charlotte," she said. "I have a project."

"That's fantastic," I said. "I am in fact a professor in the United States too."

"Are you considering a master's degree here in the program?"

I looked at her dumbly.

"The Icelandic studies master's?" she said. "Are you not thinking about enrolling in the program?"

Indeed I was not thinking of it, and I had not heard of it. "I've already got a job," I said. "I'm here because I'm curious."

"I am a professor in North Carolina," she said again. "I have a project here. Why are you here if you don't have a project?"

"Ah, hello, Mr. Caswell," Ólöf said walking up behind Professor North Carolina and saving me from a further beating. "Welcome. I am ready to show you around."

Professor North Carolina scowled at me. "Now I take myself out of it," she said, then turned and walked away.

"Nice to meet you," Ólöf said.

"Very nice to meet you too," I said.

"It is not open to the public," Ólöf said, trying to explain.

"It's all right."

"Please," she said. "Come in and follow me, please. I will show you a few of our treasures, as you requested."

Walking through those locked doors felt like entering the Cheyenne Mountain Complex at NORAD, which I have never done. There were desks and telephones and stacks of books and people hurrying about with a look of urgency, a bustling lair of activity devoted to studying and preserving and safeguarding these treasures of Iceland, which are, indeed, treasures of the world.

Ólöf gave me a quick tour of the facility and told me about some of the programs. She mentioned the master's degree in Viking and medieval Norse studies, which the institute offers in partnership with the University of Iceland, as well as universities in Denmark and Norway. I had to admit, it did sound appealing. As a repository, Ólöf told me, the institute houses some of the oldest and most important manuscripts ever written in Iceland, as well as copies of those manuscripts made over the past several hundred years, and then studies of the manuscripts written during various periods. And some of those studies are about previous studies. So, the institute is made up of old books, and also books about those books, and even books about the books about the books.

Then Ólöf gave me a brief history of Iceland as a nation of the book and explained how the institute was seated at the center of Icelandic culture. The Norse people who settled here were lovers of poetry, since poetry was a gift from the god Óðinn, she told me. Poets memorized and recited or sang their poems and the poems of others, so there was little need for writing and books. Iceland adopted Christianity at the Alþingi in AD 1000, and it caused no great disturbance, for practitioners of paganism and its great pantheon of gods were happy to adopt yet another god to invite help and guidance. Christianity is a literary faith, a faith of the book, and under Christianity it became fashionable for the sons of Icelandic chieftains to study for the priesthood and be ordained. These early ordained priests held on to their knowledge and love for the poetry and stories of the past, many of which were rooted in paganism. "Thus the culture which came with Christianity acquired a national character," writes Kristjánsson in *Iceland and Its Manuscripts*, "and secular rulers, with their knowledge and love of the ancient poems and stories, became at the same time masters of a literary culture."

As masters of a literary culture, early in the twelfth century, learned men began to write down the ancient poems and stories they had long revered, along with histories of the country, opening the way for what is sometimes referred to as the Age of Writing. In mainland Europe, Christian writers always wrote in Latin, "but in Iceland," Kristjánsson writes, "the art of writing was taken into the service of the native culture, and nearly all Icelandic authors wrote in their mother tongue [Icelandic], not Latin." This helps explain why writers from that time, like Snorri Sturluson, were Christian but writing the stories and poems and history of a fading pagan cultural past.

This Age of Writing was a time of great productivity and attention to recording the stories that made Iceland the country it is, and without the devotion and forward thinking of these early writers, we wouldn't know much about the Norse people during this time. Remarkably, because the Icelandic language has changed so little over the past one thousand years, Icelanders today can still read even the oldest Icelandic texts.

The institute is named after Árni Magnússon (1663-1730), who was born in Iceland but lived much of his life in Denmark. He assembled one of the greatest collections of rare books and manuscripts the world has known, and he had a particular fondness for books and manuscripts written during the Age of Writing. Iceland was ruled by Denmark from 1380 to 1944, and by the time Magnússon started collecting, many of the medieval manuscripts written in Iceland had already been brought to Copenhagen. Magnússon collected a great many more, and he borrowed and had copied the books he desired but was unable to purchase. Part of Magnússon's collection was lost during a fire in Copenhagen in 1728 (which destroyed 28 percent of the city), just two years before he died. In 1944 Iceland achieved independence from Denmark, and following years of negotiation the two countries settled on dividing the Magnússon collection between two repository and research centers: the Arnamagnæan Institute in Copenhagen and the Árni Magnússon Institute in Reykjavík.

This process was mostly completed by 1997, and in 2009 the entire collection housed between the two institutes was added to the UNESCO Memory of the World Register.

While the 1728 Copenhagen fire was likely an accident (started by a restaurant manager and his wife making candles in their flat, though they blamed their seven-year-old son), there was something to learn, I felt, about the danger of losing books and libraries to accident and war, or to a rising cultural disposition that disappears them to rewrite or bury disagreeable and embarrassing stories from our past. The books and manuscripts Magnússon lost in the fire are books and manuscripts we all lost. We lost the great *Bibliotheca Corviniana*, the Royal Library of King Matthius Corvinus of Hungary, purposefully destroyed by the Ottomans in 1526 when they sacked Budapest, a treasure of knowledge and wisdom. We lost the Royal Library of Antioch, destroyed in AD 363 by Jovian, the Christian emperor of Rome, for its many books he regarded as unholy. But violence against books is not locked in our past only. It is ongoing, even today. In the twenty-first century we have yet to see the kind of book-burning campaigns like those of the Nazis, but political and social movements routinely attempt to ban books from public schools and libraries, and writers once touted by American university English departments are intentionally disappeared from course reading lists.

Ólöf led me deeper into the institute and showed me a vault, a climate-controlled room protected by a massive door, with a second massive door behind it. A lock panel on the wall required two keys stored in separate lockboxes. Ólöf swung the great outer door open, unlocked the inner door, and said, "Wait here." She opened the inner door just enough to slip inside.

A minute or two later she emerged with a book in her hands. "This is a copy of the *Prose Edda* of Snorri Sturluson, copied down by Jakob Sigurðsson in 1765," she said. "This book came from Canada, from Gimli, Manitoba. You see, many Icelanders immigrated to Canada, especially southern Manitoba, because it has a climate similar to ours. It

Ólöf led me deeper into the institute and showed me to the vault.

is familiar, like a home. The book is called the Melstradirs Manuscript, after the farm family who possessed it at one time."

Ólöf told me that many of the oldest books have names. Each book has a title, of course, but it also has a name. Titles travel with the content no matter the edition, but these names are unique to a specific volume, unique to an individual book. The name helps identify the book and say something of its history, as the books are often named by the place they were written, or by the place they were housed or stored, or by someone who housed or stored them. A book may be named after its writer, or the person who copied it, though often the author is unknown.

"We have up to eighteen thousand manuscripts housed here," Ólöf told me. "It was once true that researchers focused on the authors of the books, but so little could be known about them. The new research is not concerned with authors at all but with the manuscripts themselves as distinct objects. Especially since the authors are not very much on the page."

I thought of Jane Smiley's introduction to *The Icelandic Sagas*, where she makes a similar claim: the sagas are "a literature in which individual authors seem to disappear, while the voice of an entire way of life seems to speak distinctly." Ólöf went on to tell me that because the author is not important in this new scholarship, "a single manuscript is a representation of the time or the moment the manuscript was written or copied. Each manuscript is unique, but we have to look at them as a whole too. The manuscripts are changing over time as they age, and the changes are part of their story, but just as the manuscripts change, we are changing the way that we read them."

Then she looked at me as if slightly embarrassed. "But I do not know very much. I am not a researcher. I am just a librarian."

I thought then about *Gilgamesh*, the oldest written story in the world, an archetype for the journey of a human life, and yet we do not know who wrote it. And *Beowulf*, whose writer does establish a presence on the page here and there but is still unknown. And the great body of stories told and kept by Indigenous cultures worldwide, all without a unique author. Then I remembered one of my complaints about creative writing programs in the United States: they seem to want to convince you that you matter as a writer, that you need to learn how to be a writer, as opposed to learning how to do the writing for the benefit of the reader. Such programs, as I have experienced them, teach you that the writer leads and the reader follows. They are abuzz with who published what where, who won which prize, and whose name is highly touted, not necessarily by readers but by all the other writers chasing after that highly touted name. But in the cases of *Gilgamesh* and *Beowulf*, and many of the Icelandic sagas, it's the reader who reads and so keeps the stories alive. In the process of time, it matters less and less who wrote the book; what matters is that we have the story.

"Do you happen to have a reading room?" I said. "I'm wondering if I might be able to have a look at one of these manuscripts on my own. If I could spend a little time with one or two of them?"

"No," Ólöf said. "That would be quite impossible. But one moment." She slipped behind the door again. "Let me show you something else."

She showed me a manuscript of Icelandic sagas from the vault dated 1510, but the date was uncertain. "This manuscript was copied out by Jón Ólafsson of Grunnavík," she said, "which is up in the Westfjords near Hornstrandir."

"Ah, yes," I said. "I was up in the Hornstrandir a number of days ago."

"Já," she said, sucking in her breath.

The manuscript's cover was made of wood and bound by cordage. Ólöf opened it to show me some of the vellum leaves, which were a deep, dark brown, almost translucent, and lighter in color toward the center of the pages. I knew from my studies in book history that vellum stored for centuries in the damp dark of medieval stone buildings darkens like this over time, and from the smoke and soot of the warming fires burning in the rooms where they were written or copied. Even from my vantage several feet away, the ink appeared to be raised up off the leaves so as to give it a roughened texture over the perfectly smooth vellum, almost like braille. My observations were affirmed later when I read in P. A. Baer's review of *The Manuscripts of Iceland*, "The vellum pages of these manuscripts tend to be very dark and the pigments of their illustrations are often not as bright, but the ink, especially after the fifteenth century, is black, shiny, and easy to read because it lies so thickly on the vellum that it almost stands out in relief."

Like the manuscript Ólöf held open for me now, the most valuable and revered medieval manuscripts housed at the institute are written on vellum leaves, and vellum is not paper. Having read David Diringer's exhaustive work, *The Book before Printing*, I knew that paper was invented in China around AD 105. It is made by felting and then drying individual plant fibers that have been crushed and suspended in water. The word "paper," however, comes from *papyrus*, a plant that once grew in abundance on the banks of the Nile. Before the invention of paper, ancient Egyptians laminated strips of the inner fibers of papyrus with wheat paste and vinegar to make sheets suitable for writing and painting. These sheets became known as papyrus. In fact, the Ancient Greek word for this inner fiber is *bubloi*, and the writing on papyrus is known as *biblos*, and, in Latin, *biblia*, the origin of the word "Bible."

Vellum is something else entirely. It is made from calfskin that is prepared by washing and divesting it of hair, then soaking the skin in lime and stretching it on a wood frame. The skin is then scraped clean on both sides (the hair side and the flesh side), pounded with chalk, and rubbed smooth with pumice. The skin is left on the frame to dry before being trimmed and turned into leaves to make books. "Leaves" is the appropriate word, as "page" indicates one side of a book's leaf. The flesh side of the vellum leaf is a bit lighter in color than the hair side, and the tradition was to place the flesh sides side by side in books, and the hair sides as well, for aesthetic consistency. It was expensive to make vellum, so medieval writers were fond of using abbreviations and symbols to save space. One of the largest of the medieval manuscripts written in Iceland, the *Flateyjarbók* (a book of Icelandic sagas so called because it was written and housed on the island of Flatey, where Scott and I spent the night), required the skins of 113 calves.

Some scholars make a distinction between parchment and vellum, and others do not. Vellum is made exclusively with calfskin, and parchment may be made using the skins of cattle, sheep, goats, and even deer. Calfskin is considered of finer quality for writing than the skins of other animals, and the thinnest and best vellum leaves were made from the skin of an aborted calf, called uterine vellum. Diringer is among the scholars who claim the two words are synonymous, and in his book he makes this boast: "Parchment [vellum] was, of course, the most beautiful and suitable material for writing or printing upon that has ever been used."

Vellum is not just beautiful and suitable; it is also highly durable (unlike paper), which is one reason these books have survived for so long. Another testament to these medieval writers is that they made very durable inks. A typical Icelandic ink recipe calls for bearberry extract and willow sap rendered into a viscous and rather sticky goo. Medieval writers

"The *Codex Regius* is my favorite. It is our jewel."

used quill pens, and in Iceland they mostly used quill pens made from swan feathers, cut from the left wing to fit perfectly in the right hand.

Ólöf showed me several more books, each time disappearing into the vault and returning with a new volume. She showed me some pages from *Íslendingabók* (Book of Icelanders) and a manuscript about knights from what she termed "the Arthurian literature." She told me to wait a moment and went down a hallway into another part of the institute. She returned with a stack of brochures and monographs.

"These are for you," she said, handing them to me. "For your study. If you come back with a project, we will welcome your research here. Now I will have to get back to my desk."

"May I ask you one more question?" I said.

"Yes, of course."

"What is the most important book housed here?"

"They are all very important," she said.

"Okay, then, what is your personal favorite?" I asked.

"My favorite? I am not a researcher. I am just a librarian. I do not have a favorite." She paused a moment. "Well, in fact I do. I must say that the *Codex Regius* is my favorite. It is the closest to us Icelanders. It is our jewel."

I had seen the *Codex Regius* on display at the Culture House in Reykjavík a few days earlier, but its home is at the institute. Except for the approximate date the *Codex Regius* was written (1270), nearly nothing can be known about the manuscript's story before it was acquired by Brynjólfur Sveinsson, the bishop of Skálholt, who inscribed on it the date 1643. Sveinsson held onto the book for nearly twenty years and then in 1662 offered it to the Danish king, Frederick III, who ruled over Iceland. It then became known as the *Codex Regius*, or the King's Book, and was housed in the Royal Library in Copenhagen. In 1971 Denmark returned the book to Iceland after a long negotiation, along with some eighteen hundred additional manuscripts.

The *Codex Regius*, sometimes called the *Poetic Edda* and also the *Konungsbók*, or by its shelf mark number GKS 2365 4°, has no known author or authors and was likely copied from older sources written between 1200 and 1240. The manuscript consists of forty-five vellum leaves and eight more that have been lost. It is the oldest collection of Eddic poems, and many scholars regard it as the most important. Certainly it is the most famous; when Denmark returned the manuscript, it was transported on a ship with armed escort and welcomed by a grand ceremony like a hero home from the wars. The manuscript's thirty-one poems are at the wellspring of our understanding of pagan Norse mythology, which includes the heroic deeds and adventures of Óðinn, Þórr, and Loki. These poems tell of the creation of the cosmos out of chaos and the establishment of Ásgarðr, as well as the prediction of the loss and destruction of that creation during Ragnarök, from which the Earth will rise again, cleansed, from the sea.[38]

It made good sense that Ólöf would name the *Codex Regius* as her favorite, for in so many ways it is at the center of what Iceland was and so at the center of what it has become and will be. I recalled something that former Icelandic president Finnbogadóttir had written in her preface to *Iceland and Its Manuscripts:* "The Icelanders [preserved] these national treasures through centuries of poverty, and in doing so have kept alive both the Icelandic language and a cultural identity."

I thanked Ólöf several times on my way out, grateful for all that I had seen.

That Day on Viðey

AROUND REYKJAVÍK

My time in Iceland was at an end, and I thought I'd get out of the city before my flight by taking the one-kilometer ferry ride to Viðey, which in 1856 Lord Dufferin described as "a beautiful little green island where the eider ducks breed, and build nests with the soft underdown plucked from their own bosoms." It sounded weirdly inviting, even heavenly, with all those nests and feathers and ducks, and as the island was no longer inhabited, it promised a solitary walk over its network of trails.

On my walk to the ferry terminal, I saw three hairless dogs walking on leashes and a hairless cat sitting in a window. A couple pushed a stroller past me down the quay with a little someone inside hooked up to an oxygen tank. It was a bright, clear day, and as I walked the ferry terminal seemed to be moving away from me. When at last I arrived, I waited for the ferry with three men traveling with a woman who was dressed in cut-off jeans and a dirty sweatshirt, her lower lip pierced, her calves and shins scratched up and cut in long blood-red lines. I felt embarrassed for her somehow and looked away into the water around the dock to find it filled with ghostly jellyfish, translucent parachutes with four darker rings at their centers.

Later I would identify them as moon jellies, fairly common, of the genus *Aurelia*. What was going on in these waters, I did not know, but

Ghostly jellyfish, translucent parachutes each with four darker rings at center.

high concentrations of jellyfish with few to no other marine species can be a sign of low levels of oxygen in the water due to pollution, environmental degradation, and climate change. In coastal areas, especially, low oxygen can be caused by agricultural runoff and the warming of the oceans. As we heat the Earth's atmosphere by burning fossil fuels, much of that heat is absorbed by our oceans, and warmer ocean water stores less oxygen. Many marine species can't survive in low oxygen, but jellyfish can.

The story gets stranger still, as at least one species of jellyfish (there may be others) is capable of regenerating itself. *Turritopsis dohrnii*, sometimes called the immortal jellyfish, can revert to an earlier stage and start its life cycle all over again. Unless it is killed by some trauma, it can potentially live forever, like elves. Imagine if a butterfly, instead of dying, could return to its larval stage, move into a chrysalis again, and reemerge as a butterfly. Or if a chicken could return to its egg and hatch again. Or if an eighty-year-old man could return to age sixteen for a do-over. If we keep heating the planet, we'll find more and more jellyfish taking over warm coastal waters, and if these jellyfish can live forever, they may just take over the world's oceans, perhaps alongside AI taking over from humans on the continents. Standing on the dock watching those jellyfish, I realized how tired I was of waiting for the world to end.

But the sun was out and sparkled on the waters, and I still wanted to spend the day walking on this green island, so I got on the boat with half a dozen other people.

Landing on Viðey, I walked the path to Viðey House and Viðey Church, remnant ghosts of a time long gone. Viðey House was completed in 1755 as the plush residence of the treasurer of Iceland, Skúli Magnússon. The church was completed not long after at Magnússon's behest. The residence was occupied by various other well-to-dos over many decades and, along with the church, is now a modest attraction for tourists and the one place on the island you can get a nice coffee. As this boatload of travelers were all headed to the coffee shop, I lit out onto the trail headed southeast toward Þórr's Headland and the abandoned fishing village at the island's tip. I was going to walk all the way around the island and maybe have a coffee after.

The trail led me to Skúli's Hill, the island's highest point (32 m), whose sheer side is known as Death Slope. I suppose death is possible if you fell from this slope, but it didn't look promising. Better to keep walking and move happily and easily along the trail, the green grasses running in the wind, the soft sun falling over everything. I could see Reykjavík across the bay waters and hear some of the low murmuring of the annoying industrial world, ships and engines and babies and things, but it was quiet and green and easy like a Wordsworth poem, and I really liked it. I could see why a man like Magnússon, who controlled the nation's coffers, might find a way to convince the country to build him a big stone home and a church so he might live a little way off from the bustle of the

Fairies live here, hidden in these low hills, but I saw only birds.

growing town. I imagine he enjoyed retreating to his island, as even in his time the news cycle caused anxiety, fear, and a general sense of dissatisfaction. In our time, we know that the endless and overwhelming stream of information coming from our electronic devices defeats the imagination and slaughters the mind, and the only way to heal yourself is to unplug. An island like Viðey, like Iceland, has long been a place beyond places, one of refuge and renewal.

Headed south along the trail, I came into the area known at the Women's Hiking Hills, whose south end is an old sheep pen and a stone cave. A story persists that fairies live here, hidden in these low hills and under dwellings, but I saw only birds: redshank (*Tringa totanus*), purple sandpiper (*Calidris maritima*), northern fulmar (*Fulmarus glacialis*), and common eider (*Somateria mollissima*).

The eider, sometimes called the eider duck, holds a special value here on Viðey and in Iceland more broadly, as the bird is the source of eiderdown, harvested for pillows and comforters for the past thousand years. Its lightness and supreme insulating properties made it ideal for bedding during the age of settlement, and its natural scarcity made it so valuable that it was accepted as payment by medieval tax collectors. In the twenty-first century, far more gold and diamonds are produced annually than eiderdown, making it the province of royalty and the super-rich: an eiderdown pillow (with no pillow cover) runs $2,600 to $5,000, depending on size and firmness, and a queen-size comforter costs $7,200 to $11,000, depending on how warm you want it.[39]

Goose down and feathers used for costuming, hats, and other ornamentation are generally collected when the birds are killed for meat, or by plucking them while still alive, an unconscionable practice known as live plucking. But eiderdown in Iceland is harvested by collecting abandoned eider nests, nests the female eider makes to incubate her eggs by plucking the soft underfeathers from her own breast; in other words, she live-plucks herself. The eider is a ground nesting bird, highly vulnerable to predators, which in Iceland is largely the arctic fox. After the eggs hatch, the mother leaves the nest and leads her ducklings onto the water for better protection, which of course means facing predators that come from beneath. The nest can then be harvested, cleaned, and made into eiderdown. Eiders happily nest near human habitation, which foxes tend to avoid, and Icelandic farmers realized long ago that the more they did to protect eiders from foxes, the more nests they could collect. A kind of symbiosis developed between human and duck. As Lord Dufferin put it, "After the little ones are hatched, and their birthplaces deserted, the nests are gathered, cleaned, and stuffed into pillow-cases, for pretty ladies in Europe to lay their soft warm cheeks upon, and sleep the sleep of the innocent." What is good for the eider, of course, is not necessarily good for the fox, as one of the ways to protect the eider is to kill foxes—bullets, poison, traps. There is a skeleton in almost every closet.

Walking in that open land toward the abandoned fishing village beyond Þórr's Headland, I realized I missed the smell of pines in the mountains of my homeland, but here on Viðey I had the sea air and the grasses and flowers, bright stars in all that green. I walked easily until I noticed someone walking in front of me; I was catching up.

At the footings of some of the village houses long gone, I stood back, but not too far back, from the person I had caught up to as we both read the historical signs. She looked over at me through the tumult of her long red curls, and I noticed her red freckles. Her black walking boots looked more suited to a much tougher trail. She smiled warmly and introduced herself as Dorian from Switzerland.

"What do you think," she said, not really looking at me. "What a world used to be here, hey?"

"What a world," I agreed. "All these homes and people's lives once here, now gone." I thought of the eiders abandoning their nests.

"The cod fishery collapsed, I guess," she said. "People had to leave."

"And all that's left are these ruins to mark their passing."

She nodded. "I'm remembering Anaïs Nin. Something like, we don't see what is there; we see who we are."

"You're a reader," I said.

"Of course. Are you headed this way around the island?" she asked.

"I am," I said.

"Shall we walk around the island together?"

"Of course," I said.

I walked with Dorian, wading through the tall grasses where the trail narrowed, and we rounded the island tip to make our way up the east side. She was quiet and easy to be around, and we instantly became friends. I followed her more than she followed me, she moving fluidly through the high grasses of late summer along the island edge and through the rough patches of yellow wildflowers, and white ones, maybe daisies. I thought about the fairies living among the hills I had passed through, and about Shakespeare's Ariel in *The Tempest*. I thought about how an island is a

I walked
with Dorian,
wading
through
the tall
grasses,
and we
rounded
the
island
tip.

container, even a prison like Alcatraz, whose edge is not a fence but a flat plain of barrier waters. But an island is also a place of possibility where seemingly most anything might happen. We walked together up to the isthmus, around the big pond, and around the north end of West Island before turning south toward Viðey House. When we eventually crossed back to Reykjavík on the boat, maybe we'd have dinner together, and maybe we would wander the streets in the night lit by the summer sun. Maybe. A couple of days from now I would board my flight and return to my home country, and she to hers, and that would be all, each to the other a memory, a texture, a pleasant disturbance.

When we weren't talking as we walked, I was thinking about how you want to forget some things in your life, and forgetting them helps you a little farther on your path, but your memory reaches back despite your will, sometimes by way of places you know best and sometimes by new places like this one, to recover what you wished not to remember—people, events, feelings you like having forgotten. You surprise yourself revisiting the past this way when memories arise that you didn't remember you had. But all of it is illusion, because the you of that past is gone, and you cannot become who you once were, just as you cannot really forget what you have seen and experienced. What we all want is to belong, to belong somewhere, some time, and perhaps belong to someone, even if only to ourselves. You can travel a long way and not ever see what you came to see, because what you came to see is not why you went. You travel by instinct and intuition, turning this way and that by what attracts you as you go, and the journey through all your days feels messy, disorderly, turbulent, a source of some agitation and discomfort. But it is this turbulence you live by. You bring it up from the center to the heart, like nutrients through the stem of a flower.

I came to think of this walk, and this fine journey to Iceland, as my own most crowded hour. Walking all these kilometers through Iceland with Scott, these few with Dorian, and the many kilometers I walked alone, I was reminded that the veil between this world and the next is thin, and it really may be possible to speak to the dead. Later, after I left,

I would lose a friend to cancer, but in his absence I would hold on to his firm belief that what matters in a life is that you be of some good use, that you be of service, that you help. And in order to help, you must first seek to answer a few essential questions, questions you need to ask repeatedly across the journey of your life: Who am I? What do I mean in the world? What am I going to do? And with whom am I going to do it?

Acknowledgments

Several of these essays first appeared together as a column at *McSweeney's Internet Tendency*. I am grateful to *McSweeney's*, and to John Warner, my editor there.

My journey in Iceland was supported by a research and travel award from the Office of Research and Innovation at Texas Tech University. Both the university and the Texas Tech Honors College (where I teach) subsequently awarded me faculty development leave to write much of this book. I am grateful and fortunate to work at a university that so readily supports and believes in the humanities as essential to the academy and the foundation of civil society. Thank you.

A number of people I met during my travels were generous and helpful while I was in Iceland, and many of them were helpful to my research later. Chiefly among them, my gratitude goes to Ólöf Benediktsdóttir, librarian at the Árni Magnússon Institute; Jón Þorsteinn Sigurðsson, for his stories and guidance in the highlands of Iceland; and Ester Rut Unnsteinsdóttir at the Arctic Fox Center.

Karen Oslund at Towson University, whose excellent book *Iceland Imagined: Nature, Culture, and Storytelling in the North Atlantic* was an essential guide during my research, read sections of my work in progress and offered many excellent suggestions and corrections. My gratitude, too, goes to Steven Churchill at Duke University for his book *Thin on the Ground: Neandertal Biology, Archaeology, and Ecology* and for answering my questions about Neandertals.

I am grateful to animator Siggi Orri Þórhannesson, my seatmate on the flight home from Iceland; and to filmmaker Simon Chan of Banana Planet Films for answering my questions about artwork and illustration.

As always, I am grateful to everyone at Trinity University Press, especially this book's editor, Steffanie Mortis, who took a chance on this boisterous telling of the journey I made in Iceland.

A number of friends stood sentinel to my work and supported me throughout the writing process, and to them I am most grateful: Ray Harrison, Michael San Francisco, Derek Sheffield, Jim Warren, and Chris Witmore. I am indebted to my ophthalmologist, Dr. Kelly Mitchell, and to Darla Probst, certified ophthalmic technician, without whom I would not have been able to see well enough to write this book.

I am indebted to Scott Dewing, as always, for the journey we made together, for wise counsel and guidance during rougher waters, for consistency and discipline, and for brotherhood. We've been friends nearly since the beginning, and we will be friends all the way to the end.

I have long admired illustrated books and have long imagined writing a book worthy of illustration. It's been my great pleasure and privilege to work with artist Julia Oldham. The book is vastly improved by her contribution, and I've gained a new friend.

And to Taylor Johnson, who read and commented on portions of this book, gave me the phrase "vast and bulky," suggested this book's title, and encouraged and supported my steady hours at labor, often in very close quarters in my truck camper, I am forever grateful.

Notes

1 While Albert speaks the first profane word in this book, I suspected that most of the profanity is spoken by Scott. It made sense, then, for Scott to conduct a "data analysis and breakdown of profanity usage" (his phrase). The results are as follows: Albert—*shit* = 1; Sean Connery—*fuck* = 1; Caswell—*damn* = 3, *shit* = 6, *fuck* = 3; Dewing—*damn* = 6, *shit* = 18, *fuck* = 13.

2 See Theroux's interview with Andrew McCarthy, "I Hate Vacations," published in the *Atlantic* (September 2013).

3 Not to be confused with the *Sun Voyager*'s artist, Árnason, whose name is barely distinguishable.

4 The average annual rainfall in Reykjavík is thirty-one inches. By comparison, Seattle, Washington, gets about thirty-seven inches of rain a year.

5 I packed these books around for six weeks only to give them away to people I met just a few days before departing for home.

6 Not unlike thirteenth-century Icelandic poet Snorri Sturluson's *Prose Edda*, written to instruct young poets, which I discuss in the chapter "On Not Looking into Snorri's Pool."

7 In this chapter I have borrowed a few lines from a towering giant of a travel book, *Travels with a Donkey in the Cévennes*, by Robert Louis Stevenson. It's like a word find, only with sentences. Additionally, the title is an allusion to John Keats's great poem "On First Looking into Chapman's Homer."

8 Known as the innsog, or ingressive sound, it is offered as agreement and to encourage a speaker to keep talking. The innsog is common

to northern Germany, Ireland, across Scandinavia, and places in the Canadian Maritimes.

9   John Keats died of tuberculosis at the age of twenty-five, so all his sonnets might be considered early.

10   Since you are probably wondering, the whale shark is the biggest fish in the world, topping out at 61.7 feet long.

11   An often quoted but never sourced description of Hákarl.

12   Chestnut set this world record in 2020 after our journey in Iceland, breaking his own world record. He also held the record when Scott and I traveled there.

13   Here Scott and I discovered the perfect companion to the pylsur, a porter by Viking Brewery called Black Death (not to be confused with Brennivín, also known as Black Death). The label features a skull in a top hat between two electric guitars with the suggestion to "Drink in Peace."

14   Puffins were easy to catch in nets like butterflies.

15   In 1960 a husband and wife team, Helge and Anne Stine Ingstad, discovered the first Norse settlement site in North America at L'Anse aux Meadows, Newfoundland, verifying the account in the *Grœnlendinga Saga*. See *The Viking Discovery of America* (2000), coauthored by the pair, and Anne Stine Insgstad's great *The New Land with the Green Meadows* (2000).

16   For more about Egevang's work, see *Bird of the Sun: A Photographic Tribute to a Bird on the Wing* (2009) and "Arctic Tern: Extreme Migration from Pole to Pole," available at carstenegevang.com.

17   Surely someone has thought of this already, but if not, may I have credit for that name?

18   Two fantastic books on the subject are Søren Thirslund's *Viking Navigation* (2013) and Leif Karlsen's *Secrets of the Viking Navigators* (2018), in which the author describes sailing his own long ship from Norway to Iceland.

19   The study also finds that due to a shorter heel, modern humans are better at long-distance running than Neandertals. See David A.

Raichlen, Hunter Armstrong, and Daniel E. Lieberman, "Calcaneus Length Determines Running Economy: Implications for Endurance Running Performance in Modern Humans and Neandertals," *Journal of Human Evolution* 60, no. 3 (March 2011).

20 Bronowski is writing about the Bakhtiari tribes of Persia, who were and are nomadic pastoralists, hence the reference to summer pastures. I have taken some liberty with Bronowski's work to liken some of the cultural characteristics of these modern pastoral nomads to Neandertals, who would not have kept sheep and goat herds but hunted wild game herds in the landscape they found themselves in.

21 Trolls are notably not Christianized and hate churches and monasteries. They are among the few pagan holdouts from the Viking world.

22 The cow became Drangey Island. The female troll is the sea stack next to Drangey, and the male troll was turned into a stone that has since eroded away.

23 In medieval Europe, a baby born inside its caul was considered lucky and destined for greatness. Likewise, possessing a caul would bring its bearer good luck. Cauls were prized by sailors as a talisman against drowning, as the baby born inside the caul had come into the world underwater (still inside amniotic fluid). Sailors paid large sums of money for a baby's caul.

24 Vatnajökull covers 8,100 square kilometers, which is about 8 percent of the entire country.

25 This happened again on our bus ride to Egilsstaðir. The bus pulled into a small town and stopped at a red light. I happened to look out the window and, to my horror, the Netherlander materialized at the crosswalk. He looked right at me.

26 On YouTube, search for "Lake monster seen in Iceland original HQ uncut version."

27 Similar to Smaug in Tolkien's *The Hobbit*. Tolkien was deeply influenced by Icelandic folktales and sagas, as well as Iceland's landscape, as a model for Middle Earth. See also Wagner's *Ring Cycle*

opera, based on Norse myths and unsurprisingly similar to *The Lord of the Rings*.

28 Icelandic news sources have taken issue with this story, remarking that Friends of Lava is an environmental group and that reports that they are organized around support for huldufólk are spurious.

29 Tolkien's character Gollum in *The Hobbit* and *The Lord of the Rings* is eerily similar to Shakespeare's character Caliban in *The Tempest*.

30 In *Letters from Iceland*, Auden claims that in Iceland "any average educated person one meets can turn out competent verse."

31 Formerly fishing and fish products; aluminum smelting is also in the top three.

32 He had a point. In *Letters from Iceland*, Auden reports that the longest word in Icelandic is Vaðlaheiðarvegavinnuverkfærageymsluskúrs-lyklakippuhringurinn. Translation: "a latch-key belonging to a girl working in the office of a barrister."

33 Later I would travel to the interior of Iceland and gaze upon the mountain where a rock giant lived.

34 There is a female equivalent, the clitoris bone, certainly a compelling subject for a future essay.

35 To get to my room, I had to drop through a hole cut in the living room floor and covered by a round hatch. It was like entering a submarine.

36 People said eagles followed Horace everywhere he went, though he said this was not true. At a weeklong event in Oregon, he gave a talk to a large audience. As he spoke, someone pointed up at three eagles flying high overhead.

37 It is a coincidence that my guide's name was also Jón.

38 Two more excellent sources are *A History of Icelandic Literature*, edited by Daisy Neijmann (2006), and the digital archives available through the Árni Magnússon Institute.

39 To learn more about eiderdown, you can't do better than Edward Posnett, "The Weird Magic of Eiderdown," *The Guardian*, July 19, 2019.

KURT CASWELL is a writer and professor of creative writing and literature in the Honors College at Texas Tech University, where he teaches intensive field courses in writing and leadership. His books include *Laika's Window: The Legacy of a Soviet Space Dog, Getting to Grey Owl: Journeys on Four Continents,* and *In the Sun's House: My Year Teaching on the Navajo Reservation* (all published by Trinity University Press). He is also the author of *An Inside Passage,* which won the 2008 River Teeth Literary Nonfiction Book Prize. His essays and stories have appeared in the *American Literary Review, McSweeney's, Ninth Letter, Orion, River Teeth, Terrain,* and the *International Journal of Travel and Travel Writing.* He lives in Lubbock, Texas.

Printed in the USA
CPSIA information can be obtained
at www.ICGtesting.com
JSHW011304170923
48582JS00002B/2